Professional Driver's Guide

by
B. A. THOMPSON

FCInstT, TEng (CEI), FIRTE, FRSA

Edited by
Colin Clark

AM Inst TA, AMCIT

CRONER PUBLICATIONS LIMITED

CRONER HOUSE
LONDON ROAD, KINGSTON UPON THAMES,
SURREY KT2 6SR
TELEPHONE 081-547 3333

Professional Driver's Guide

First Edition
February 1971

Second Edition
September 1973

Third Edition
February 1975

Fourth Edition
February 1977

Fifth Edition
June 1979

Sixth Edition
March 1982

Seventh Edition
April 1985

Eighth Edition
December 1986

(Revised reprint July 1987)

Ninth Edition
September 1988

Tenth Edition
June 1991
© Croner Publications Ltd 1971, 1986

ISBN 1 85524 096 3

Printed in Great Britain by
Whitstable Litho Printers Ltd., Whitstable, Kent

CONTENTS

DRIVING ON MOTORWAYS

PART THREE—IN TRANSIT AND OFF THE ROAD

LOADING REGULATIONS

PARKING, LOADING AND UNLOADING

VEHICLE MAINTENANCE

TESTING AND INSPECTION OF VEHICLES

11

Users of this book should be aware that only Acts of Parliament and statutory instruments have the force of law and that only the courts can authoritatively interpret the law. The publishers give no warranty as to the accuracy of the information in this work.

Please also note that throughout this book, for the sake of simplicity, the word "he" is used to represent both male and female gender.

INTRODUCTION

The current legislation based on road safety demands much of both the operator and driver of all types of motor vehicles.

To the person at the wheel these demands are most exacting and require considerable skill and practical knowledge, particularly with the driving of commerical vehicles where the responsibilities are much greater.

In addition to the required driving skills, a driver is also expected to acquire a good general knowledge of the various orders and regulations and how to apply them. It is, therefore, most necessary that drivers of today be classified and trained as the "professionals" that they really are. To this end both government and industry actively encourage driver training facilities, including the Young HGV (now Large Goods Vehicle [LGV]) Driver Training Scheme whereby young persons between the ages of 18 and 21 are allowed to train as LGV drivers.

Employers, trade unions and associations are assisting in improving conditions in which drivers may acquire additional knowledge to cope with their obligations.

The need for higher standards of road safety to satisfy industrial requirements is fully recognised. Increases in the numbers of vehicles far exceed the supply of "qualified" drivers. Better education of all road users is the biggest and most essential factor in the reduction of accidents.

It would be difficult to find an industry which, in one form or another, is not involved in the use of motor transport, whether under own control or hire purchase or loan agreement, for the distribution of its goods or the carrying of passengers. In addition to the drivers necessary to fulfil these requirements, there are the sales and service representatives and owner drivers who are also dependent on the motor car to efficiently fulfil their services.

Professional drivers are skilled drivers with high standards of accident free driving and courtesy, but they and their future professional colleagues require much more information and training in the legal and documentary obligations placed upon them.

The aim of this book is to assist all drivers of motor vehicles, whether they are drivers of cars, vans, goods or Special Type carrying vehicles by putting into plain language an outline of the comprehensive and complex regulations to which they are subject. It can also serve as a textbook for training and study purposes for those who are intending to embark on a career in the transport industry.

Information concerning the standard car driving test is not included as it is considered that, in general, users of this book would already have taken the standard test. For this reason detailed references to road procedure and road signs are omitted as these are amply covered by the Highway Code and textbooks on basic driving instruction.

In order to keep the information to reasonable proportions and in "layman's" language, detailed references to acts, orders and regulations are omitted. If readers wish to improve their knowledge of transport law or the various statutory instruments, the use of the companion book, *Croner's Road Transport Operation*, is recommended.

To assist the reader in the use of this book the contents have been divided into five parts and the various applications and responsibilities have been progressively listed in the appropriate parts.

The fourth part of the book has been devoted to continental transport, very much a part of commercial vehicle activities through its support of exports, and knowledge of this subject is considered necessary for the progressive training of the professional driver.

B.A. THOMPSON

PART ONE
THE LAW'S DEMANDS

THE DRIVER'S RESPONSIBILITIES

The provisions of the Transport Act 1968 to which has been added European Community legislation require a driver to:

(a) see that the vehicle which he drives is in a fit and serviceable condition

(b) comply with the regulations governing driving and the use of goods vehicles with respect to loading and unloading

(c) comply with the regulations in respect of drivers' hours and the keeping of drivers' hours of work records.

The employer and/or owner driver is also responsible for seeing that these requirements are properly carried out. Infringement of any of these regulations can result in a fine and/or loss of the operator's licence, also endorsement or disqualification of a driving licence, with possible loss of employment for the driver.

THE LICENSING SYSTEM

The licensing system for goods vehicles, known as operator licensing, is governed by the Transport Act 1968 and mainly affects the employer. However, drivers should be aware of the implications attached to this legislation as it affects day to day operations. The main points are:

(a) vehicles not exceeding 3.5 tonnes gross vehicle weight used for carrying goods are exempted from all forms of licensing restrictions. These vehicles are not required to display an operator's licence and drivers of such vehicles do not have to keep records. However, there is an exception to these rules: if the vehicle tows a trailer and if the combined gross weight of the vehicle and the trailer exceeds 3.5 tonnes the driver has to keep a record of his working hours, which means that the vehicle should be fitted with a tachograph for this purpose (see page 53 for information on tachographs)

(b) vehicles exceeding 3.5 tonnes gross vehicle weight require an operator's licence to enable the vehicle to be legally used on the road and this is either a *restricted* licence for use on own account operations or a *standard* licence for hire and reward. The standard licence will specify whether international and national operations are permitted or national operations only. The latter restricts the carrying of goods to within Great Britain

(c) operator's licence discs are provided for motor vehicles, but **not** for articulated trailers. The disc must be displayed in the cab of the vehicle. The discs are coloured to denote the type of operation covered thus **orange** denotes a restricted licence, **blue** a standard licence, **green** a standard international licence and **yellow** an interim licence.

The disc is not normally issued until the vehicle has been in the company's possession for one month but the vehicle can be driven without the licence disc displayed during this period.

Since June 1984 environmental considerations have affected the granting of operators' licences because the Licensing Authority has the power to attach conditions to it on environmental grounds. Such conditions may include restrictions on movement, eg vehicles may only operate from and to a depot between certain hours of the day and on certain days of the week; the route between the depot and the nearest main road may be stipulated so that residential areas are avoided; vehicle noise must be kept to a minimum, ie no revving of engines in the early morning, etc. Whilst these requirements are the concern of the employer, it is up to the employee to see that any instructions received on such matters are strictly complied with, as any infringement may result in the employer being called before the Licensing Authority to explain why the conditions are not being met.

PART TWO
ON THE ROAD

THE DRIVER

ACCIDENTS

One of the requirements outlined in the *Highway Code* (but never sufficiently appreciated by the driver) is the information that must be given in the event of an accident. The following procedure should be adopted.

Stop:
1. If any persons are injured seek assistance and send for an ambulance and the police.
2. Try to obtain witnesses.
3. Exchange particulars with the driver of any other vehicle involved, ie:
    - (a) the name and address of the driver
    - (b) the owner's name and address if the driver is not the owner
    - (b) the registration number of the vehicle, its type and colour
    - (c) the name and address of the relevant insurance company.

Indicate:
4. The extent of any damage sustained.
5. The time the accident occurred.
6. Where the accident occurred, ie:
    - (a) the locality
    - (b) the names of streets and roads adjacent
    - (c) the position of the vehicles at the time of the accident
    - (d) the visibility at the time of the accident.
7. The cause of the accident (include any information on whether signals were given).

Provide:
8. A rough sketch to emphasise the general situation.

All drivers obviously hope that they will not be involved in an accident and are therefore content to leave any consideration of this procedure until one occurs.

It is accepted that drivers, experienced or otherwise, may become nervous and excited when involved in an accident. It is essential, however, that the correct information is obtained *at the time of the accident*. Once the involved parties have dispersed the true facts can never be recalled. This is particularly stressed so that the driver appreciates the important role of factual information in negotiation between insurance companies.

When involved in an accident do not admit responsibility for the accident to the other party or to witnesses; leave this for the appropriate authorities to decide.

It should be noted, however, that the law requires a driver to stop and report any damage caused to property on or adjacent to the road or injury to certain animals as a result of an accident, to any person having reasonable grounds for requiring such information. If this cannot be done immediately then the police must be informed as soon as possible and in any case within 24 hours of the occurrence.

In the context of the above, *property* means street furniture, ie traffic signs, bollards, etc, garden walls, fences, etc and *animal* means horses, asses, mules, cattle, sheep, pigs, goats or dogs.

Failure to stop or to report an accident is an offence and where reporting to the police is concerned this should be done as soon as possible; any delay (within the 24 hour period) may still bring prosecution if it is considered that the accident could have been reported earlier.

Accident forms
It is customary for insurance companies to issue accident forms and drivers should see that they regularly carry and understand them as it will serve as a useful guide for obtaining the required information.

Production of insurance certificates

Where a driver is required to produce a vehicle insurance certificate at a police station, there is no obligation for him to produce it "in person", the legal requirement is satisfied simply if the certificate is produced. Also, the time limit for producing the document is "within seven days", however, if it cannot be produced within this period a defence is provided in the Road Traffic Act 1988 if it can be shown that it was produced at the police station as soon as possible, or, due to unforeseen circumstances, it was not reasonably practicable to produce the certificate before the day on which proceedings for non-production were started.

DRIVING LICENCES — GENERAL

Qualifying for a licence

A driving licence may be obtained if, during the past 10 years, the applicant has:

(a) held a full licence

(b) passed the test

(c) held a full licence issued in Northern Ireland, the Isle of Man or the Channel Isles.

Types of Licence

1. Provisional licence
2. Ordinary driving licence *(issued before June 1990)*
3. Unified driving licence *(issued from June 1990)*
4. Heavy Goods Vehicle (HGV) licence *(issued before April 1991)*
5. Public Service Vehicle (PSV) licence *(issued before April 1991)*
6. Visitors driving licence
7. International driving permit

Following harmonisation of the driving licensing system within the European Community a unified driving licence was introduced into the United Kingdom on 1st June 1990. From that date "groups" of vehicles for driving test purposes were replaced by "categories" and all new licences issued will show the categories of vehicles the licence holder is entitled to drive.

Holders of the "ordinary driving licence" retain all their rights under this new system (but see page 36) and need take no action to have this licence replaced unless circumstances require particulars shown in the licence to be altered, ie change of name or address, etc. If the licence has to be amended in some way then a new unified licence will be issued in its place.

Changes have also occurred to vocational licences, ie HGV/PSV licences and these changes took effect from 1st April 1991. Here again drivers holding a HGV and/or PSV licence need not surrender the licence, or licences, until they expire but when they apply for renewal they will receive a new licence in the unified format which will contain details of *all* their entitlements in one document. (See pages 25–32 for details concerning large goods vehicle entitlements.)

A provisional licence must be obtained in order to take a vehicle on the road for the purpose of learning to drive and take the regulation test.

The holder of a provisional licence may drive a vehicle only when accompanied by, and under the supervision of, a qualified driver that is a person who is at least 21 years of age and who has held a full licence for at least three years.

The vehicle must display "L" plates at the front and rear.

Application forms for a licence are obtainable from post offices.

Vehicle Categories
The categories of vehicles for driving test purposes are as follows:

Category A *(Group D before change)*
Motorcycle (with or without sidecar) but excluding vehicles in category K or P. (Additional categories covered — B1 and P).

Note: provisional licence holder may not carry a pillion passenger even if that person is a qualified driver.

Category B *(Groups A, B, [Group B limited to vehicles with automatic transmission] before change)*
Motor vehicle with a maximum authorised mass not exceeding 3.5 tonnes and not more than 8 seats in addition to the driver's seat, not included in any other category and including such a vehicle drawing a trailer not exceeding 750kg authorised mass. (Additional categories covered B + E, B1, C1, C1 + E, D1, D1 + E, F, K, L, N and P).

Note: a category B test must be passed or a full ordinary licence must be held before application can be made for provisional entitlement to drive a vehicle in catgegories C, C + E, D and/or D + E.

Category B1 *(Group C before change)*
Motor tricycle with an unladen mass not exceeding 500kg and with a maximum design speed exceeding 50km per hour but excluding vehicles in categories K, L or P.

Category C *(HGV classes 2 or 3 before change)*
Goods vehicle exceeding 3.5 tonnes maximum authorised mass (permissible maximum weight*) including such a vehicle drawing a trailer not exceeding 750kg maximum authorised mass (maximum gross weight*) or a trailer of any weight having a single axle.

Category C1 *(Groups A or B, before change)*
Goods vehicle exceeding 3.5 tonnes but not exceeding 7.5 tonnes maximum authorised mass including those drawing a trailer not exceeding 750kg maximum authorised mass. (Additional¹ categories covered — B, B + E, B1, C1 + E, D1 + E, F, K, L, N and P.)

Category D *(PSV classes 1, 2 and 3 before change)*
Passenger vehicle having more than 8 seats in addition to the driver's seat including such a vehicle drawing a trailer not

---

* "maximum authorised mass" in relation to a goods vehicle has the same meaning as "permissible maximum weight" in s. 108 (1) of the **Road Traffic Act 1988,** and in relation to any other vehicle or trailer as "maximum gross weight" in regulation 3 (2) of the **Road Vehicles (Construction and Use) Regulations 1986** (SI 1986 No. 1078).

exceeding 750kg maximum authorised mass (maximum gross weight*) of a trailer of any weight having a single axle.

Category D1 *(Groups A or B, before change)*
Passenger carrying vehicle (not used for hire or reward) with more than 8 but not more than 16 seats, in addition to the driver's seat, and including such vehicles drawing a trailer not exceeding 750kg maximum authorised mass. (Additional categories covered — B, B + E, B1, C1, C1 + E, D1 + E, F, K, L, N and P).

Category B + E *(Groups A or B, before change)*
Combination of a motor vehicle in category B and a trailer with a maximum authorised mass exeeding 750kg.

Category C + E *(HGV Class 1 before change)*
Goods vehicle in category C drawing a trailer exceeding 750kg maximum authorised mass and having more than one axle; articulated goods vehicle.

Category C1 + E
Combination of a motor vehicle in category C1 and a trailer with a maximum authorised mass exceeding 750kg but up to an overriding maximum not exceeding 7.5 tonnes.

Category D + E *(PSV classes 1 and 2 before change)*
Passenger carrying vehicle in category D drawing a trailer exceeding 750kg maximum authorised mass and having more than one axle.

Category D1 + E
Combination of a motor vehicle in category D1 and a trailer with a maximum authorised mass exceeding 750kg but up to an overriding maximum not exceeding 7.5 tonnes.

Category F *(Group F before change)*
Agricultural tractor but excluding any vehicle included in category H. (Additional category covered — K.)

---

* "maximum authorised mass" in relation to a goods vehicle has the same meaning as "permissible maximum weight" in s. 108 (1) of the **Road Traffic Act 1988,** and in relation to any other vehicle or trailer as "maximum gross weight" in regulation 3 (2) of the **Road Vehicles (Construction and Use) Regulations 1986** (SI 1986 No. 1078).

Category G *(Group G before change)*
Road roller.

Category H *(Group H before change)*
Track laying vehicle steered by its tracks.

Category K *(Group K before change)*
Mowing machine or pedestrian controlled vehicle.

Category L *(Group L before change)*
Electric vehicle. (Additional category covered — K.)

Category N *(Group N before change)*
Vehicle exempted from duty under s.7 (1) of the Vehicles (Excise) Act 1971.

Category P *(Group E before change)*
Moped.

A test passed on a vehicle with automatic transmission restricts driving to that type of vehicle. A further test must be taken before driving a vehicle with manual transmission.

A test passed on a moped does not entitle the candidate to a full motor cycle licence.

A test passed on a moped or motor cycle does not entitle the candidate to drive a motor car or heavy motor car.

It is an offence to drive a vehicle on a public road unless the driver holds the appropriate licence for that particular class of vehicle.

The cost of an ordinary driving test is currently £21.50. For a test conducted on a Saturday the fee is £35.

To obtain a refund of the test fee in the event of having to cancel the test ten clear working days notice must be given.

Minimum age limits

Small passenger vehicle carrying not more than nine persons	17 years
Small goods vehicle not exceeding 3.5 tonnes permissible maximum weight (including the weight of any trailer drawn)........................	17 years

Medium sized goods vehicle not exceeding 7.5
tonnes permissible maximum weight (including
the weight of any trailer drawn) and not
adapted to carry more than nine persons .... 18 years
Other motor vehicles, ie goods vehicle exceeding
7.5 tonnes permissible maximum weight
(including the weight of any trailer drawn);
articulated vehicle .... 21 years
Agricultural tractor — specially licensed as such
and not exceeding 2.45m in width .... 16 years
Road roller: up to 11,690kg unladen weight .... 17 years
over 11,690kg unladen weight .... 21 years

The age limits do not apply to vehicles owned or driven
under order of HM Forces.

Cost and duration of licence
Full driving licence £17
Provisional licence (valid until the holder's 70th
birthday) with conversion to full licence after
passing driving test £17
Duplicate licence £5
A new licence issued to a driver following
   (a) disqualification for certain drinking and
     driving offences £20
   (b) for other disqualifications £5
Large goods vehicle (LGV) entitlement* £10
Large goods vehicle (provisional) entitlement
(valid for six months) £5

All licences (including LGV entitlement) are issued by the
Driver and Vehicle Licensing Centre (DVLC) Swansea SA6
7JL.

Renewal and replacement
A driving licence must be renewed on or before the date of
expiry. No days of grace are allowed. A licence lost or

---

* from 1.4.91 *Large Goods Vehicle* entitlement incorporated into Unified Driving
Licence and valid until holder's 45th birthday or for 5 years whichever is longer.

defaced may be replaced at a cost of £3 and HGV licences or LGV entitlement, at £5.

Endorsement and disqualification

If a licence is endorsed or the driver is disqualified he must inform his employer. The unified driving licence or ordinary driving licence should be produced at a magistrate's court for endorsement, not the HGV licence (if applicable). If he is disqualified from driving (*which means driving any vehicle on a public road*) and he also holds a HGV licence he must **surrender this to the DVLC Swansea.** At the end of the period of disqualification he can apply to the DVLC for the return of his HGV licence or LGV entitlement.

Note: the DVLC can order the driver to take another LGV test if they consider that the circumstances warrant it.

Production of licence

A police officer can demand the production of a driving licence for examination and if it is not immediately available it is a defence to show that the driver (a) produced it at a police station nominated by him within seven days, or (b) he produced it there as soon as possible, or (c) due to circumstances it was not reasonably practicable to produce the licence before the day on which proceedings for not producing the licence were commenced.

Remember!

A driver must have a current licence, which must be signed. This is a legal requirement.

DRIVERS' LICENCES — LARGE GOODS VEHICLE (LGV) ENTITLEMENT
(*formerly Heavy Goods Vehicle [HGV]*)

From 1.4.91 the term "Heavy Goods Vehicle" was replaced by "Large Goods Vehicle" (LGV) for driver licensing purposes, also from that date responsibility for issuing entitlement to drive large goods vehicles passed from licensing authorities to the Driver and Vehicle Licensing Agency (DVLA) at Swansea although licensing authorities (now referred to as Traffic Commissioners) retain certain powers which are discussed in more detail later.

The rights of existing holders of HGV licences are fully preserved under the new system and in fact Class 3 holders gain from the change in that they can now drive any rigid goods vehicle and all HGV licence holders may also drive large passenger vehicles, ie vehicles with 17 or more seats, excluding the driver's seat, provided not more than 8 passengers are being carried and the vehicle is not used for hire or reward.

Drivers obtaining vocational entitlement and those seeking to renew their licences will now receive one document in the form of a unified licence which will contain details of all the categories of vehicles they are entitled to drive (see pages 20–23 for list of categories). The LGV entitlement will last until the driver reaches the age of 45 or for 5 years, whichever is longer. From age 45 a driver will need to supply a medical report each time he applies to renew his entitlement.

It is an offence to cause or permit a person to drive a large goods vehicle unless the driver holds the appropriate entitlement.

A large goods vehicle is defined as:

(a) an articulated vehicle*

(b) a large goods vehicle, ie a motor vehicle (not being an articulated vehicle) constructed or adapted to carry or haul goods and having a permissible maximum weight (including any trailer drawn) exceeding 7.5 tonnes.

Qualifications for entitlement

Anyone who applies for LGV entitlement must show that:

* an LGV entitlement is not required where the total permissible weight does not exceed 7.5 tonnes, or the tractive unit of which does not exceed 2.05 tonnes unladen weight.

26

(a) he holds a Group A ordinary driving licence or a unified licence for category B entitlement

(b) he is at least 21 years old (but see under (e) below) at the starting date of the licence

(c) he is free from any disease or disability including defective eyesight (but see page 33) which is likely to affect his driving large vehicles which might be a danger to the public.

(d) he is not suspended or disqualified from holding LGV entitlement

(e) he is a young LGV driver undergoing approved training (see page 35)

(f) he has passed the LGV driving test of the appropriate category.

Categories of large goods vehicle entitlement

There are two categories of large goods vehicle entitlement:

Category C — rigid goods vehicle exceeding 3.5 tonnes maximum authorised mass (which is the same as "permissible maximum weight" for goods vehicles) including towing a trailer up to 750kg maximum authorised mass ("maximum gross weight" for trailers) or any trailer with one axle. **Note:** this category entitlement allows vehicles exceeding 7.5 tonnes maximum authorised mass to be driven but the weight and size of trailer allowed to be towed is limited.

Category C+E — goods vehicle in category C drawing a trailer exceeding 750kg maximum authorised mass and having more than one axle; articulated goods vehicle.

Holders of category C or C+E entitlements (or HGV licences) may also drive large passenger carrying vehicles (PCVs) having 17 or more seats in addition to the driver's seat, provided they carry not more than 8 passengers and the vehicle is not being used for hire or reward.

To qualify for category C entitlement the test must be

passed in a goods vehicle exceeding 7.5 tonnes maximum authorised mass (mam), and for category C + E entitlement the test may be passed in either an articulated vehicle or drawbar trailer combination. A drawbar trailer combination must be at least 15 tonnes permissible maximum weight. (Tests taken from April 1994 will have to be in goods vehicles of at least 11 tonnes mam for category C and either articulated vehicles of at least 21 tonnes mam or drawbar trailer combinations where the trailer has at least two axles, one being a steering axle, and a wheelbase of at least 4 metres and the whole having a permissible maximum weight of at least 21 tonnes for category C + E entitlement).

Application for licence and test

To obtain a provisional large goods vehicle licence the driver must supply the following documents —

(a) his ordinary Group A (or Group B for automatics only) licence, or a full category B entitlement, or test pass certificate for category B and the provisional licence;

(b) completed application form D2;

(c) completed medical report — form DTp 20003

which should be sent, together with the appropriate fee, to the Driver and Vehicle Licensing Agency (DVLA), Swansea.

The application can be made up to three months before the licence is required to commence. Medical reports may be completed by a registered doctor up to four months before the licence is requested to commence.

The medical examination must be paid for by the driver, however certain disabilities will preclude the granting of LGV entitlement including —

(a) an epileptic attack since attaining the age of 5

(b) abnormal eyesight

(c) insulin treated diabetes.

(In the case of drivers holding HGV licences abnormal

eyesight or diabetes may not necessarily preclude them from continuing to hold the licence or seek renewal of their entitlement when their present licence expires — see page 33).

When the provisional entitlement has been issued the driver may commence to drive large goods vehicles of the category covered provided he is accompanied by a qualified driver and the vehicle displays "LGV" "L" plates, one at the front and one at the rear.

LGV driving test

Application for a test should be made on form DLG26 which is obtainable from post offices and local Department of Transport offices.

The current fee is £48 (£75 if the test is conducted on a Saturday) which must accompany the application and can be made to any office of the Driving Standards Agency at least 28 days before the day the applicant wishes to take the test. If the applicant has to cancel the test for any reason five clear working days notice must be given otherwise the test fee is forfeited.

A vehicle suitable for the test and in the category for which the test is to be conducted must be provided by the applicant. The vehicle must be unladen and have an enclosed cab.

Note: if a driver for the LGV test holds a category B entitlement for vehicles with automatic transmission the LGV test can be taken in a vehicle with either manual or automatic transmission. If the test is taken in a vehicle with manual transmission the restriction on the category B entitlement will be removed.

Hints and tips

1. One of the requirements that the examiner will be looking for is "vehicle sympathy" and the driver should ensure that the vehicle he uses on test is in first-class condition. Things such as steering, brakes, gears and clutch should operate freely in order that he may properly demonstrate the handling of these components.

2. **If using a vehicle fitted with a two-speed axle, the driver should make sure that he understands and can demonstrate the correct change procedure — see instruction on the two-speed axle, page 122.**

3. The road test lasts about 1½ hours and may seem to be the least exacting part of the test, but old habits die hard and some drivers may find it difficult to do the "right" things while carrying out what is, to the professional, an automatic function. Particular attention should therefore be paid to distance, speed, gear changing and signals when overtaking, as the examiner will be looking for near perfection.

4. Two points will certainly be covered during the oral part of the test
   Q. What exercise do you complete to ensure that the king-pin locks are home and locked?
   A. Engage first gear and attempt to pull away with the trailer wheels still braked.
   Q. What is the last thing you check before you move off?
   A. That the correct number plate is on the back of the trailer.

5. Included in the safety questions are: "What would be the cause of black smoke emitted from a vehicle's exhaust and what would you, as a driver, do about it?". "Worn or dirty injectors" would satisfy the first part and "take the vehicle out of service" would be enough to satisfy the second.

6. It is advisable to study the Highway Code and to know about warning devices common to air pressure braking systems.

Competent drivers who are careful and considerate need have no worries but, as the Department of Transport booklets emphasise, a test should not be applied for unless the applicant is reasonably certain of his competence. Drivers should cross-check their own assessments with someone who can give an honest and useful opinion of their driving ability.

The Test

The driving test will last for about 1½ hours over about 25 miles and will consist of

1. A test of the driver's ability to manoeuvre a vehicle in a confined space. This part of the test may take place on or off the public highway.

2. A drive over a route comprising various types of road including fast open roads, urban roads and varying traffic densities.

3. An oral test of the driver's knowledge of the Highway Code, and of his knowledge of those components of the vehicle affecting its safe operation, and other functions including safe loading and distribution of the load.

Applicants for the test must provide a vehicle of the appropriate category, unladen and having an enclosed cab. In addition to the examiner, any person authorised to attend the test for supervision purposes must also be allowed to travel in the vehicle.

Duration of LGV entitlement

On passing the test the LGV entitlement will be included in the unified driving licence and this part of the licence is valid until the holder's 45th birthday, or for 5 years whichever is longer. From age 45 onwards LGV entitlement is renewable every 5 years and medical reports are required with each application. From age 65 the entitlement is renewable each year.

Cost of LGV entitlement

Provisional — £5
Full — £10
Reinstatement of entitlement following disqualification — £5
Exchange (removal of endorsements, claiming or applying for additional entitlement) — £5

Holders of Class 1, 2 or 3 HGV licences

Existing holders of the HGV driver's licence (issued before 1.4.91) may continue to drive heavy goods vehicles until the licence expires and holders of Class 3 or Class 3 "restricted" licences may now drive any rigid goods vehicle. Also, all HGV licence holders are permitted to drive large passenger carrying vehicles, ie vehicles with seating for 17 or more passengers in addition to the driver, provided the vehicle is carrying not more than 8 passengers and is not being used for hire or reward.

Licence renewals

To renew the licence application must be made on the reminder form DLG1RC which will be sent to the driver's last notified address, or the application form D2 (either will be acceptable) and sent to the DVLA, Swansea (not to the licensing authority as in the past) accompanied by —

(a) the ordinary driving licence or unified driving licence (if already issued)

(b) HGV licence

(c) form DTp 20003 medical report (if aged 45 or over)

(d) the correct fee.

The DVLA will either replace all existing licences with one unified licence, or if the unified licence has already been issued, the LGV equivalents of the HGV classes will be added to it. (If a driver also holds a PSV licence this can be sent at the same time so that the passenger carrying vehicle (PVC) entitlements can be included). In either case one of the following appropriate LGV categories will be shown (see pages 20–23 for complete description of all categories):

LGV category shown on licence	Original HGV class
C, and C + E (limited to drawbar trailer combinations only)	2 or 3
C, and C + E (limited to drawbar trailer combinations only and in both cases limited to vehicles with automatic transmission)	2A or 3A
C + E	1
C + E (limited to vehicles with automatic transmission)	1A

Thus drivers in classes 1 or 2 lose none of their entitlement and class 3 drivers gain entitlement under the new system.

Medical standards

Under the new system certain medical conditions have been included in the regulations as "relevant disabilities" although they have always been included in the list of disabilities in the guidance notes for doctors. These "relevant disabilities" are —

Insulin treated diabetes — diabetics receiving insulin treatment may not be issued with vocational entitlement. It is a question of fact as to whether this condition exists and entitlement will be refused as a matter of law. However, drivers suffering from diabetes and who declared their condition to the Traffic Commissioner before 1st January 1991 may continue to drive provided they have been issued with, or have been allowed to retain their licence.

Eyesight standards — as for diabetics some concessions have been made and drivers who obtained a vocational licence before 1.1.83 and who still hold their licence on 1.4.91 may qualify for entitlement on lesser standards, ie having a visual acuity of not worse than 6/12, on the Snellen Scale, in the better eye and not worse than 6/36 in the other eye. If glasses or contact lenses are worn the uncorrected acuity in each eye must be not worse than 3/60.

Existing monocular drivers, provided they declared their condition to the Traffic Commissioner before 1.1.91 and have been issued with a licence or allowed to retain their existing licence, may continue to drive and have their entitlement renewed. They must, however, have a visual acuity of not worse than 6/9 in their remaining eye (or 6/12 in the case of drivers issued with a licence before 1.1.83). If this acuity deteriorates they will have to stop driving large goods vehicles and/or large passenger vehicles.

Notification of illness or disability

It is a requirement of the law that if an illness or disability develops, or worsens, which is likely to affect a person's driving, the Drivers Medical Branch, DVLA, Swansea SA99 1TU must be notified, unless the disability is not expected to last for more than three months.

Traffic Commissioners

In the past the licensing authorities have been responsible for issuing HGV licences and dealing with disciplinary matters as regards these licences. With the changes brought about by the new system they are now only responsible for issuing duplicates of HGV licences lost or defaced. However, whilst they no longer issue new licences they retain certain powers as regards dealing with matters of conduct under the title of Traffic Commissioners.

The Secretary of State for Transport, through the DVLA, is responsible for issuing all entitlements and he will only grant LGV entitlement provided he is satisfied that the applicant is a fit and proper person. If there are any questions relating to a person's conduct, whether he is a new applicant or an existing holder of a HGV licence or LGV entitlement, he can refer the matter to the Traffic Commissioner for deliberation.

The Traffic Commissioner can require the applicant for, or the holder of a licence or entitlement, to provide him with any information and if necessary appear before him to answer any questions concerning his conduct. Failure to comply with any requests made by a Commissioner can result in the application being refused, or in the case of an existing licence holder, the Commissioner can determine whether the licence should be revoked or suspended, and if revoked, for what period of time. Any decision made by a Traffic Commissioner is binding on the Secretary of State. The Commissioner must also make his decision known to the applicant, or holder of a licence or entitlement.

If a person wishes to appeal against a decision made by the Secretary of State to suspend or revoke the licence on grounds of his conduct or physical disability, or to disqualify him because of his physical disability he can appeal to a magistrates' court (or to a sheriff, if in Scotland) in the area in which he lives. He must, however, notify the Secretary of State of his intentions, and also the Traffic Commissioner if he was involved in the decision.

34

If a court, or sheriff, makes an order on the appeal it is binding on the Secretary of State.

Disqualification

If a driver is disqualified from driving by a Court he loses entitlement to drive any motor vehicle on a public road. It does not matter what vehicle he was driving at the time of the offence. However, if the disqualification applies only to category C entitlement this will not necessarily debar a driver from retaining his category B entitlement.

Application for the reinstatement of a licence can be made after a certain period of time depending on the length of the disqualification (see page 75). The reinstatement of category C entitlement will be considered at the end of the period of disqualification.

The Secretary of State can refuse to reinstate that part of the licence until the driver has passed a large goods vehicle driving test.

Production of licence

A police officer or a DTp examiner can demand the production of a driver's licence and in the case of an examiner can also require the driver (of a goods vehicle) to sign his (the examiner's) record sheet. They may also require the driver to state his date of birth.

If the licence cannot be produced on demand it may be presented at a police station (of the driver's choice) within seven days or as soon as reasonably practicable thereafter. In the case of a DTp examiner the holder has up to ten days or as soon as reasonably practicable thereafter, in which to produce the licence either at the examiner's office or at a specified traffic area office.

It is an offence not to produce a licence when required or within the specified periods or fail to state date of birth.

Young LGV drivers

A goods vehicle drivers training scheme is in operation to

encourage young persons between the ages of 18 and 20 to obtain trainee LGV driving licences.

Provided they hold a clean ordinary or unified driving licence for Group A or B, or category B entitlement and they enter into an agreement with an approved employer, they can learn to drive large goods vehicles commencing with category C vehicles.

Progression from category C to category C + E can be made 2 years from the date of passing the category C test when the LGV trainee drivers full licence will act as a provisional entitlement to drive vehicles in category C + E.

A trainee may not drive vehicles in category C + E until reaching the age of 21, except under supervision.

The trainee licence can be withdrawn if the driver is convicted of road traffic offences which result in his ordinary licence or unified (category B) licence being endorsed with more than three penalty points.

Passenger carrying vehicles

Whilst the emphasis of this book is aimed at the professional goods vehicle driver, some drivers may drive large passenger carrying vehicles from time to time, ie vehicles with 17 or more seats in addition to the driver's seat, not used for hire or reward.

At present such vehicles can be driven by the holder of an ordinary driving licence issued on or before 31.5.90 provided they are aged 21 or over, and this practice can continue until 31.3.92 by which time they will have had to decide

(a) whether to apply to take a passenger carrying vehicle (PCV) test which will also include a medical report (form DTp 20003) to obtain a full category D entitlement, or

(b) to seek restricted entitlement to drive any rigid PCV not used for hire or reward.

In the case of (b) no driving test will be necessary but the driver will have to provide a statement on form DTp 20005 that he has driven such vehicles regularly in the three years prior to making the application, and he will also need to include a medical report on form DTp 20003. The full PCV driving entitlement fee will have to be paid.

The fee for a PCV driving test is £45.
The fee for PCV entitlement (full or restricted) is £22.50.
Medical reports must be paid for by the applicant.

To gain category D entitlement the test must be passed in a vehicle having an overall length of at least 8.5m (from 1.4.94 the vehicle will have to be at leat 9m in overall length).

DRIVERS' HOURS (Goods Vehicles)

The working hours of drivers are strictly controlled by legislation and European Community (EC) law prevails for the majority of commercial operations. Where vehicles, or the type of work being carried out, are exempt from EC law, British regulations, in the form of the Transport Act 1968 as modified, apply. If journeys are made to countries outside the European Community either the domestic laws of the country concerned must be adhered to, or if the country is a party to the European agreement on international road transport (AETR) those rules must be followed.

The regulations can be briefly summarised as follows.

1. EC Regulation 3820/85 applies to drivers operating commercial vehicles exceeding 3.5 tonnes maximum permitted weight when engaged on journeys within the United Kingdom or to or from other Member States of the European Community (these are known as Community regulated journeys), ie Belgium, Denmark, Eire, France, Germany, Greece, Italy, Luxembourg, the Netherlands, Portugal and Spain.

2. AETR rules apply to drivers operating commercial vehicles exceeding 3.5 tonnes maximum permitted weight

to countries which are outside the EC but are a party to the AETR agreement, ie Austria, Czechoslovakia, Norway, Sweden, USSR and Yugoslavia.

3. British Domestic legislation applies to drivers who drive vehicles exempt from the EC rules including vehicles not exceeding 3.5 tonnes maximum permitted weight.

4. Mixed driving is where a driver changes from driving under EC rules to driving under British rules and vice-versa.

In the following pages each set of rules is given in detail.

Drivers of vehicles used by the armed forces, police and fire brigades are exempt from the regulations as also are drivers when driving vehicles completely off the public road system.

A driver is anyone who drives a vehicle, either regularly or occasionally, or is carried on the vehicle in order to be available for driving if necessary; part time drivers such as maintenance staff and technicians or employees who have to use a goods vehicle as a means of transporting themselves and equipment or carrying out errands in the course of the owner's business.

Offences

It is an offence to contravene any part of the drivers' hours regulations and heavy fines can be imposed on a driver (up to £1000) if convicted. In addition to the driver being fined the employer may also be prosecuted and in very severe cases the employer can face a prison sentence — in these circumstances the operator's licence may also be put at risk.

It is, therefore, very important for a driver to fully understand the rules governing his working hours so that infringements are avoided.

Prohibition of certain types of payment

Under EC law it is an offence for payments in the form of bonuses, etc to be made for distance travelled and for the amount of goods carried if this is likely to endanger road safety.

1 — Community Regulated

EC Regulation 3820/85 applies to drivers of vehicles exceeding 3.5 tonnes permissible maximum weight (including the weight of any trailer drawn) used for carrying goods, whether laden or unladen, within the United Kingdom or to or from another Member State of the European Community (this is known as "Commnity" regulated journeys) unless the vehicle or the operation is exempt. (A list of the exemptions is given on pages 42–45.)

In conjunction with the above-mentioned regulation, EC Regulation 3821/85 also applies and this is concerned with the use of techographs and the charts which must record drivers' working hours. Details of these regulations will be found on pages 53–64.

Daily driving period
This is a maximum of **nine hours** which may be extended to **10 hours** maximum not more than twice a week.

The daily driving period is defined as being the period between any two daily rest periods or between a daily and a weekly rest period.

Weekly driving
Weekly driving is governed by the requirement that a driver must, after no more than six daily driving periods, take a weekly rest period. This weekly rest period can be postponed until the end of the sixth day if the total driving time over the six days does not exceed the maximum corresponding to six daily driving periods.

Total fortnightly driving
Total fortnightly driving is **90 hours** maximum.

Note: a driver can drive up to a total of **56 hours** in one week but is restricted to **34 hours** in the second so that over the two consecutive weeks the limit is not exceeded.

Driving time

A driver may drive for a total of **4½ hours** (which can be either continuous or accumulated) after which a break must be taken.

Breaks from driving

After not more than a total of 4½ hours driving a break of at least **45 minutes** must be taken unless the driver begins a rest period. This break can be split into breaks of **15 minutes** (if they are less than this they are not classed as breaks) each spread over the driving period or immediately following it so that they aggregate 45 minutes. If split in this way the driver must ensure that no period of driving exceeds 4½ hours in total without also having breaks aggregating 45 minutes. In other words this is a rolling period whereby the driver must look back over his driving time to see that he has not exceeded this total of 4½ hours.

Examples
1. Acceptable

2. Not acceptable.

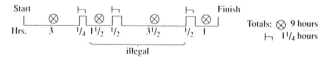

In this example the driver has not exceeded the daily driving limit, but he has exceeded the 4½ hours limit by driving for a total of 5 hours with only one break of ½ an hour.

During a break the driver must not carry out any other

work, however, waiting time and time spent in the passenger seat of a vehicle in motion, on a ferry or a train, will not be regarded as other work.

Daily rest period
In each period of 24 hours a driver must have a daily rest of at least **11 consecutive hours** which may be reduced to not less than **nine consecutive hours** on three days a week. Any reduction in the daily rest must be made up before the end of the *following week*. However, on days when the daily rest period is not reduced a driver is allowed to split this 11 hours into two or three separate periods (minimum one hour) during the 24 hours, one period of which must be of at least **eight consecutive hours**. When the daily rest is split in this manner the minimum length of the daily rest must be increased to **12 hours**.

Where a vehicle is double manned each driver must have a rest period of not less than **eight consecutive hours** during each period of 30 hours.

Daily rest periods may be taken in the vehicle provided it is fitted with a bunk and the vehicle is stationary.

Note: where journeys involve the use of ferries or trains drivers may interrupt their daily rest period, not more than once, provided they comply with the following conditions:

(a) part of the daily rest period spent on land may be taken before or after that part of the daily rest period taken on board the ferry or train

(b) the period between the two parts must be as short as possible and must not exceed one hour before embarkation or after disembarkation

(c) drivers must have access to a bunk or couchette during both parts of the rest period

(d) where the daily rest period is interrupted in this way it must be increased by two hours

(e) when time spent on board a ferry or train is not counted as part of the daily rest period it will, instead, be regarded as a break — see under *Breaks from driving*, page 40.

Weekly rest period

During each week a daily rest period must be extended into a weekly rest period totalling **45 consecutive hours,** however this may be reduced to **36 consecutive hours** if taken where the vehicle or driver is normally based, or to a minimum of **24 consecutive hours** if taken elsewhere. Each reduced rest must be made good by the driver taking an equivalent amount of rest *en bloc* before the end of the *third week* following the week in question.

A weekly rest period beginning in one week and continuing into the next can be attached to either week.

Any compensatory rest taken for the reduced daily and/or weekly rest periods must be attached to another rest period of at least **eight hours** and be granted at the request of the driver at the vehicle's parking place or driver's base.

The definition of a week is the period between 00.00 hours Monday and 24.00 hours Sunday.

Emergencies

Article 12 of the regulations allows a driver, provided that road safety is not jeopardised, to depart from the driving restrictions to enable him to reach a suitable stopping place to ensure the safety of persons, of the vehicle or of its load. In these circumstances the reason must be recorded on the tachograph chart. (*For details of the tachograph regulations see page 53.*)

Periodic checks

Article 15 requires an employer to organise work in such a way that drivers do not infringe either the hours or tachograph rules. It further requires employers to make periodic checks to ensure that the regulations have been complied with. If breaches are found steps must be taken to prevent their repetition.

Exemptions

The following are exempt from EC regulations.

1. Goods vehicles not exceeding 3.5 tonnes maximum permissible weight (including any trailer or semi-trailer).

2. Vehicles used for the carriage of passengers constructed or equipped to carry not more than nine persons including the driver (but see item 13 below).

3. Vehicles with a maximum authorised speed not exceeding 30 kph.

4. Vehicles used by or under the control of the armed services, civil defence, fire services, and forces responsible for maintaining public order.

5. Vehicles used in connection with the sewerage, flood protection, water, gas and electricity services, highway maintenance and control, refuse collection and disposal*, (this is confined mainly to collection from domestic and commercial premises, not being the result of industrial processes, it does not cover selective collection of refuse such as scrap metal, waste paper, bottles, etc which could be processed and sold) telegraph and telephone services, carriage of postal articles, radio and television broadcasting and the detection of radio or television transmitters or receivers. **Note:** Vehicles used for the carriage of postal articles on national transport operations must be fitted with a tachograph *except* for Post Office vehicles used for the carriage of letters.

6. Vehicles used in emergency or rescue operations.

7. Specialised vehicles used for medical purposes.

8. Vehicles carrying circus and funfair equipment.

9. Specialised breakdown vehicles.

10. Vehicles undergoing road tests for technical development, repair or maintenance purposes, and new or rebuilt vehicles which are not yet in service.

11. Vehicles used for the non-commercial carriage of goods for personal use.

12. Vehicles used for milk collection from farms and the return to farms of milk containers or milk products intended for animal feed.

* Some local authority operations of a commercial nature may be considered to be "in scope" of the Community regulations which means that vehicles need to be fitted with tachographs (see page 53).

In addition to the foregoing the following are exempt when operating within the United Kingdom.

13. Vehicles used for the carriage of passengers and constructed or equipped to carry not more than 17 persons including the driver, and intended for that purpose.

14. Vehicles being used by a public authority to provide public services which are *not in competition with professional road hauliers*. **Note:** vehicles falling within this description are vehicles:
    (a) being used by a health authority in England and Wales or a Health Board in Scotland or the Common Services Agency for the Scottish Health Service
    (b) providing an ambulance service under the National Health Service Act 1977 or the National Health Service (Scotland) Act 1978; or carrying staff, patients, medical supplies or equipment as part of its general duties under those Acts
    (c) being used by a local authority under the Local Authority Social Service Act 1970 or the Social Work (Scotland) Act 1968 to provide certain social services
    (d) being used by HM Coastguard; a general or local lighthouse authority; a harbour authority; airports authority within the perimeter of an airport
    (e) being used by British Rail, London Regional Transport or any wholly owned subsidiary of LRT, a Passenger Transport Executive or a local authority, for railway maintenance
    (f) being used by the British Waterways Board for navigable waterway maintenance.

15. Vehicles being used by agricultural, horticultural, forestry or fishery undertakings to carry goods within a 50km radius of the place where they are normally based, including local administrative areas the centres of which are situated within the radius. **Note:** where fishery undertakings are concerned this only applies to the carriage of live fish, or a catch which has not been processed or treated (other than frozen) from the place of landing to the place where it is to be processed or treated.

16. Vehicles carrying animal waste or carcasses which are **not** intended for human consumption.

17. Vehicles carrying live animals between a farm and a local market or from a local market to a local slaughterhouse.

18. Vehicles being used as shops at a local market; for door-to-door selling; mobile banking, exchange or savings transactions; for worship, for the lending of books, records or cassettes, or for cultural events or exhibitions. **Note:** such vehicles must be specially fitted for the use in question.

19. A vehicle carrying goods having a permissible maximum weight not exceeding 7.5 tonnes and carrying material or equipment for the driver's use in the course of his work within a 50km radius of the place where the vehicle is normally based and *provided driving the vehicle is not the driver's main activity.*

20. Vehicles operating exclusively on an island not exceeding 2300 square kilometres in area and which is not connected to the rest of Great Britain by a bridge, ford or tunnel. **Note:** this includes the Isle of Wight, Arran and Bute.

21. A vehicle propelled by gas produced on the vehicle or a vehicle propelled by electricity, having a permissible maximum weight not exceeding 7.5 tonnes.

22. A vehicle being used for driving instruction with a view to obtaining a driving licence. **Note:** this does not apply if the vehicle or any trailer or semi-trailer attached to it is carrying goods on a journey for hire or reward, or for or in connection with any trade or business.

23. Tractors used exclusively for agricultural and forestry work.

24. A vehicle propelled by steam.

25. A vehicle manufactured before 1.1.47.

2 — AETR

The European Agreement concerning the work of crews of vehicles engaged in International Road Transport, AETR, is not an EC agreement but embodies a larger group of European countries which includes the United Kingdom and other EC Member States.

Countries outside the EC which are parties to the agreement include Austria, Czechoslovakia, Norway, Sweden, the USSR and Yugoslavia and when drivers are travelling **to, through or from** these countries even though they are likely to transit an EC Member State en route, they are subject to AETR rules throughout their journey. (This means for example if a journey is made to Italy via Austria then the AETR rules apply even though the final destination is to a EC Member State.)

Drivers
Drivers of 18 and under 21 years of age may not drive vehicles, including those with trailers or semi-trailers attached weighing over 7.5 tonnes gross unless they hold a certificate of professional competence (in the United Kingdom this is the driving licence with LGV entitlement) recognised by the authorities in the countries concerned.

Driving periods
Under AETR continuous driving must not exceed **four hours,** except where the driver cannot reach a convenient stopping place or destination he may extend the driving time by not more than 30 minutes provided the daily total is not exceeded. The daily total must not exceed **eight hours** except that on two days per week it may be extended to **nine hours**; this concession does not apply to drivers of:

(a) a combination of vehicles, ie motor vehicle or tractor with more than one trailer or semi-trailer

(b) a combination of vehicles, ie motor vehicle or tractor with one trailer or semi-trailer used for the carriage of goods where the permissible maximum weight exceeds 20 tonnes.

Weekly and fortnightly driving totals
The total weekly driving must not exceed **48 hours** and **92 hours** in any two consecutive weeks.

Breaks from driving

For drivers of vehicles classified under (a) and (b) a break of at least **one hour** must be taken after the first four hours of continuous driving or **two** breaks of **30 minutes** each spread over the daily driving period in such a manner that a continuous driving period is not exceeded.

For drivers of other vehicles a break of at least **30 minutes** must be taken after four hours of continuous driving or two breaks of **20 minutes** each or three breaks of **15 minutes** each during this period or partly immediately following it.

Daily rest periods

The daily rest period must be not less than **11 consecutive hours** in a 24 hour period; this may be reduced to **nine consecutive hours** on two days per week if it is taken where the vehicle is normally based or **eight consecutive hours** on two days per week if it is taken away from the base. Any reduction in the rest periods must be made good.

If the vehicle is manned by two drivers and is not fitted with a bunk where the co-driver can rest both drivers must have a daily rest period of not less than **10 consecutive hours** during the **27 hour** period preceding any time when they were driving or doing other work. However, where a bunk is fitted in the vehicle allowing the co-driver to rest the daily rest period may be **eight consecutive hours** in a **30 hour** period preceding any time when they were driving or doing other work.

Daily rest periods must be taken away from the vehicle but where a bunk is fitted it may be taken there provided the vehicle is stationary.

Daily rest periods may be broken when the vehicle is being transported by a ferry or train (see page 41).

Weekly rest periods

A weekly rest period of **24 consecutive hours** immediately preceded or followed by a daily rest period must be taken by every crew member.

A week is any period of seven consecutive days and a fortnight any period of 14 consecutive days.

Emergencies
In the event of an emergency or in circumstances outside a driver's control the driving and rest period may be waived to allow the driver to reach a suitable stopping point or, in certain circumstances, his destination. Details of the occurrence must be noted in the record book or tachograph chart.

Record keeping
Drivers have the option of keeping records of their hours either by using the tachograph (see page 53) or individual record book but since most journeys involve transit through a Community country it is recommended that the tachograph is used. Where a control book is used the driver is limited to a daily mileage of not more than 450km (281 miles approximately) unless he is accompanied by a second driver.

3 — British Domestic Operations
Domestic legislation in the form of the Transport Act 1968 Part VI, as modified, applies to drivers of vehicles which are exempt from EC law.

Operations covered
Operations which come within the jurisdiction of British hours laws are listed below, unless they are covered by some other exemption, but it should be noted that under item 1 where a trailer is attached to the vehicle and the permissible maximum weight, ie the maximum authorised *operating* weight of the vehicle and trailer fully laden, exceeds 3.5 tonnes a tachograph must be fitted and used. In these circumstances the driver will be subject to the Community hours laws (see page 39).

1. Goods vehicles not exceeding 3.5 tonnes maximum permissible weight (including any trailer or semi-trailer).

2. Vehicles used for the carriage of passengers constructed or equipped to carry not more than 17 persons including the driver.

3. Vehicles with a maximum authorised speed not exceeding 30 kph.

4. Vehicles used by or under the control of the armed services, civil defence, fire services and forces responsible for maintaining public order.

5. Vehicles used in connection with sewerage, flood protection, water, gas and electricity services, highway maintenance and control, refuse collection and disposal, (*but see page 43, item 5*) telegraph and telephone services, carriage of postal articles, radio and television broadcasting and the detection of radio or television transmitters or receivers.

6. Vehicles used in emergency or rescue operations.

7. Specialised vehicles used for medical purposes.

8. Vehicles carrying circus and funfair equipment.

9. Specialised breakdown vehicles.

10. Vehicles undergoing road tests for technical development, repair or maintenance purposes, and new or rebuilt vehicles which are not yet in service.

11. Vehicles used for the non-commercial carriage of goods for personal use.

12. Vehicles used for milk collection from farms and the return to farms of milk containers or milk products intended for animal feed.

13. Vehicles being used by agricultural, horticultural, forestry or fishery undertakings to carry goods within a 50km radius of the place where they are normally based, including local administrative areas the centres of which are situated within that radius. **Note:** where fishery undertakings are concerned this only applies to the carriage of live fish, or a catch which has not been processed or treated (other than frozen) from the place of landing to the place where it is to be processed or treated.

14. Vehicles carrying animal waste or carcasses which are not intended for human consumption.

15. Vehicles carrying live animals between a farm and a local market or from a local market to a local slaughterhouse.

16. Vehicles being used as shops at a local market; for door-to-door selling; mobile banking, exchange or saving transactions; for worship, for the lending of books, records or cassettes; or for cultural events or exhibitions. **Note:** such vehicles must be specially fitted for the use in question.

17. A vehicle carrying goods having a permissible maximum weight not exceeding 7.5 tonnes and carrying material or equipment for the driver's use in the course of his work within a 50km radius of the place where the vehicle is normally based and *provided driving the vehicle is not the driver's main activity*.

18. Vehicles operating exclusively on an island not exceeding 2300 square kilometres in area and which is not connected to the rest of Great Britain by a bridge, ford or tunnel.

19. A vehicle propelled by gas produced on the vehicle or a vehicle propelled by electricity, having a permissible maximum weight not exceeding 7.5 tonnes.

20. A vehicle being used for driving instruction with a view to obtaining a driving licence. **Note:** this does not apply if the vehicle or any trailer or semi-trailer attached to it is carrying goods on a journey for hire or reward, or for or in connection with any trade or business.

21. Tractors used exclusively for agricultural and forestry work.

22. Public authorities' service vehicles not in competition with road hauliers. **Note:** unless covered by item 5 above, such vehicles may be subject to the Community rules (see page 39).

23. Vehicles being used by a public authority to provide public services which are not in competition with professional road hauliers. **Note:** vehicles falling within this description are vehicles:

    (a) being used by a health authority in England and Wales or a Health Board in Scotland or the Common Services Agency for the Scottish Health Service

    (b) providing an ambulance service under the National Health Service Act 1977 or the National Health Service (Scotland) Act 1978; or carrying staff, patients, medical supplies or equipment as part of its general duties under those Acts

(c) being used by a local authority under the Local Authority Social Services Act 1970 or the Social Work (Scotland) Act 1978 to provide certain social services

(d) being used by HM Coastguard; a general or local lighthouse authority; a harbour authority; airports authority within the perimeter of an airport

(e) being used by British Rail, London Regional Transport or any wholly owned subsidiary of LTR, a Passenger Transport Executive or a local authority for railways maintenance

(f) being used by the British Waterways Board for navigable waterway maintenance.

Permanent hours limits
Daily driving — 10 hours maximum
Daily duty — 11 hours maximum

A driver is exempt from the duty limit on non-driving days. This also applies to a driver who does not drive for more than four hours on each day of the week.

Driving time
Driving is time spent at the controls of the vehicle for the purpose of controlling its movement whether it is in motion or not. If some driving is done off the road, ie on a farm, at a quarry or building site, etc, this does not count as driving time but as part of the duty time.

Light vans and dual-purpose vehicles
Drivers of light vans (not exceeding 3.5 tonnes permissible maximum weight) and dual-purpose vehicles are subject only to the maximum 10 hour daily driving regulations when

engaged solely in certain professional activities, ie doctors, dentists, nurses, midwives, veterinary surgeons, commercial travellers, AA, RAC and RSAC personnel and persons using their vehicles to assist in carrying out any service of inspection, cleaning, maintenance, repair, installation or fitting. Also included are cinematography, radio or television broadcasting staff.

Emergencies

Where events cause, or are likely to cause danger to life or health of persons or animals, serious interruption in the maintenance of public services for the supply of water, gas, electricity or drainage or of telecommunication or postal services, or a serious interruption in the use of roads, railways, ports or airports, driving and duty limits may be exceeded provided the driver does not spend time on duty (other than to deal with the emergency) for periods aggregating more than 11 hours.

4 — Mixed Driving

This concerns drivers who change from community regulated operations to British domestic operations and in instances where this occurs the driver has the choice of observing the EC rules all the time, or a combination of both provided the EC limits are not exceeded when engaged on EC work. The following points must also by considered.

1. Time spent driving under EC rules does not count as "off duty" under domestic rules.

2. Time spent operating under domestic rules does not count as a break or rest under community rules.

3. Driving time under EC rules counts towards the driving and duty limits under domestic rules.

4. If any EC driving is undertaken in a week the driver must observe the EC daily and weekly rest requirements.

DRIVERS' HOURS OF WORK RECORDS

The Tachograph

Drivers who are subject to EC Regulation 3820/85 must also observe the requirements of EC Regulation 3821/85 which concerns the recording of a driver's working hours by means of the tachograph.

The tachograph is an instrument which automatically records, by means of a chart (see illustration on page 57) positioned behind the clock face, (a) the distance travelled by the vehicle, (b) the vehicle's speed, (c) the driving time, (d) the periods of work of drivers, (e) breaks in the working day and daily rest period and (f) the opening of the case containing the record chart.

It must be so constructed that the driver is able to observe that the instrument is recording properly without his having to open the case; that the last nine hours on the chart are visible to an examiner without the need for him to take any action other than opening the tachograph; and that when a second driver is carried on the vehicle his attendance is recorded on a separate chart (see illustration on page 54).

Note: If a second driver is carried in the vehicle the instrument must be capable of recording both drivers' hours of work, therefore a two man tachograph must be fitted and when the second driver commences driving the charts must be changed over to record his driving period.

On top of the instrument is the driver mode control selector with the symbols:

— Driving periods

— Working periods

— Rest periods

— Other working periods — but this symbol is not used in Great Britain

Two driver tachograph

Front View

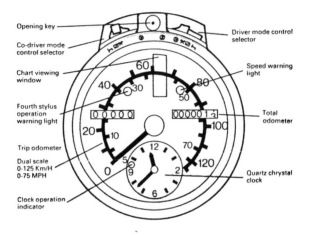

Opening key

Co-driver mode control selector

Chart viewing window

Fourth stylus operation warning light

Trip odometer

Dual scale
0-125 Km/H
0-75 MPH

Clock operation indicator

Driver mode control selector

Speed warning light

Total odometer

Quartz chrystal clock

When performing any function covered by these symbols the mode selector must be set against the correct symbol otherwise the recording on the chart will be incorrect. This is an offence which could lead to prosecution.

As an example, if, during a working day averaging nine hours, the mode selector is set on the "wheel" and is not changed, the record will show no breaks having been taken, the chart will only record that during the day the vehicle was stationary for a certain period of time. Since it is a requirement of the law that a break of at least 45 minutes must be taken after a total of 4½ hours' driving, there would be no indication from the recorded details that such a break had been observed and this would be an infringement of the drivers' hours rules which would leave the driver open to prosecution.

It is, therefore, most important that the instrument is used correctly.

Instrument checks

The instrument must be *checked* every two years and *recalibrated* every six and this work must be carried out only at an approved tachograph centre. Plaques are attached to it showing the date when the inspections are carried out. The two yearly checks are due either two years after the date shown on the installation plaque or two years after the date shown on the two yearly plaque, whichever is the later.

The six yearly recalibration is due six years after the date shown on the *installation* plaque regardless of any two yearly inspections.

At the time of recalibration all existing plaques are removed and the next inspection is then due two years hence.

In some cases the two and six yearly inspections may never be reached because if the instrument develops a fault it must be examined and repaired at a tachograph centre. When this happens a new plaque is attached to it which means that the time limits start again.

The two yearly plaque is in this format:

| TWO YEARLY INSPECTION |
| Centre/Seal No. . . . . |
| Date . . . . |

whilst the six yearly recalibration plaque is similar to this:

```
Date..............................
'I'..........................mm
'w'...............................
rev/km
                              imp/km
Seal No .......................
```

Failure to comply with these requirements carries a fine of up to £500 on summary conviction.

The chart

The chart (see illustration on page 57) is a specially wax-coated disc which comprises a centre field for recording certain particulars by hand. Radiating outwards are various concentric rings — the first being a distance (km) trace, followed by the various activity symbols, and finally the speed symbol. On the outer edge are the time segments up to 24 hours. (**Note:** there are variations in the make-up of different types of charts, depending on the make of instrument used, but the basic information remains the same.)

The distance, activity and speed traces are all marked automatically by the various styli and it is apparent from this that the mode selector referred to earlier must always be correctly positioned for the activity being carried out.

Care must be taken in handling charts as they can scratch and become damaged quite easily. By law damaged or dirty charts must not be used.

The chart must always face upwards when placed in the instrument.

Important: In some tachographs it is necessary to have a blind chart inserted when the vehicle is not in use to protect the styli from being damaged; this is because the mechanism continues to revolve whilst the clock is operating.

The instrument also has a speed warning light which allows a maximum operational speed to be set by the operator and if the limit is exceeded the warning light is illuminated. Drivers should be advised by employers if operational speeds are set. (It goes without saying that mandatory speed limits applicable to the vehicle when driven on the road should **not** be exceeded.)

Example of a completed tachograph chart

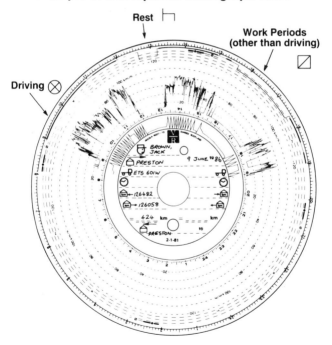

57

Drivers' responsibilities

It is the driver's responsibility to complete the charts correctly and this means that from the commencement of taking over the vehicle he must use a chart to record his driving and working time, etc. Before inserting the chart in the tachograph, the following particulars must be entered in the centre field:

(a) surname and first name

(b) the date and place of commencement of chart

(c) the registration number of the vehicle

(d) the odometer reading at the start of the first journey, etc.

At the end of the working period the centre field must again be completed by recording:

(a) the final odometer reading, which should be compared with the reading at the commencement of the chart to give the total distance travelled

(b) the place of finishing

(c) the date.

If, during a working period, a change of vehicles takes place this must be recorded on the chart (there is usually space on it to record at least two changes) and particulars of the new vehicle, together with the time of change, noted. If the second vehicle has a different make of tachograph, a chart compatible with the instrument must be used and the same procedure applied. At the end of the day all charts used must be kept together so that a complete record is available.

If some driving is done off the public highway, ie on a farm or in a quarry, this is not reckoned as driving time but as other work and the mode selector should be set accordingly — it is also advisable to make a note on the back of the chart of this type of driving should it be queried at a later date.

Whilst in charge of the vehicle the driver is responsible for seeing that the instrument is working correctly and that the mode is set properly for recording the various activities.

The time recorded on the chart must agree with the official time in the country of registration of the vehicle. (If it is an international journey the clock should be set at the official time in Great Britain and not changed on entering different time zones on the continent.) The driver must also check that the time of day is correct when placing the chart in the instrument, ie if it is 7 am the chart should not start recording from 19.00 hours.

The driver must have in his possession for possible inspection by the enforcement authorities the completed current week's charts and the chart for the last day of the previous week on which he drove. Completed charts must be returned to his employer within 21 days. Failure to return charts within the time limit is an offence and carries a heavy fine on summary conviction.

A driver must be able to produce, to an authorised examiner at any time during the prescribed period, each chart used in the tachograph. The examiner can enter the vehicle and inspect the instrument and inspect and copy or remove any charts found therein. Although there is no laid down procedure it is recommended that if a chart is removed by an authorised examiner or police officer for checking, a receipt is obtained showing the date and time of the occurrence. If a new chart has to be fitted the official should be asked to note the circumstances on that chart.

If the tachograph develops a fault or ceases to function, manual records must continue to be made of the various activities, either on the chart, on a temporary chart or a sheet of paper. Whatever method is used the original chart plus any temporary chart or sheet of paper must be kept together so that a complete record is available of the working period. On returning to the depot the employer must be notified so that arrangements can be made for repairs to be carried out at an approved centre. It is a requirement of the law that the instrument must be repaired as soon as circumstances permit. However, if the vehicle is unlikely to return to the depot within a period of one week calculated from the day of the breakdown or discovery of defective operation, the repair must be carried out en route.

When the tachograph was originally installed it will have been calibrated and sealed — there can be at least six seals attached to it — and these seals must not be tampered with. If the seals are broken for any reason the circumstances must be noted and the employer informed so that new seals can be attached by a tachograph centre (see also page 55) — *Instrument checks*).

Repairs, recalibration and sealing can only take place at an approved tachograph centre; therefore, if for any reason there is a delay in having the instrument attended to the driver should carry either a note or some advice in the cab that the vehicle has been booked in for repair on a certain date. This should satisfy an examiner if the driver is stopped during a period when manual records are being kept because of the state of the instrument.

If a chart is damaged during a working day it must not be thrown away but kept and at the end of the working period attached to the replacement chart in the tachograph.

Two or more employers

If a driver works for more than one employer he must notify each employer of the name and address of the other(s) and completed charts must be returned to the first employer irrespective of who supplied the charts.

Failure to notify each employer of the circumstances is an offence and can incur a heavy fine on summary conviction.

A driver has the right to ask his employer for copies of completed charts if he requests them.

Employers' responsibilities

It is the employer's responsibility to issue sufficient charts for the operation involved, bearing in mind the possibility of charts being damaged or removed by law enforcement officers. It is therefore a good idea to have at least seven days' supply.

The charts must be suitable for the instrument fitted in the vehicle being used. They are not interchangeable with other makes of instrument.

The employer must ensure that completed charts are returned within 21 days and the charts must be retained by him for at least 12 months and be made available for inspection by law enforcement officers if required.

All these requirements apply equally to the owner driver.

Records used in evidence
The record produced by the tachograph and any manual entries made on the chart may be evidence, and in Scotland sufficient evidence, of the matters appearing from them as they affect drivers' hours and record keeping. Other records which also show on the chart, eg a vehicle exceeding the speed limit, will not normally be accepted as evidence unless it is corroborated by other evidence such as a police patrol or radar check.

Offences
Apart from the offences already mentioned, it is an offence (a) if the vehicle to which the regulations apply does not have a tachograph, or (b) if the instrument is installed and is not being used in accordance with the regulations, eg tampering with the instrument to produce false records, etc and fines of up to £1000 can be imposed on summary conviction.

It is a defence when it is proved that:

(a) the vehicle was proceeding to a tachgraph centre for the equipment to be installed

(b) the equipment was not working correctly because it could not be repaired by an approved fitter or workshop

(c) manual recordings were being made by drivers whilst the equipment was inoperable.

Similarly, where seals are broken or removed, it is not an offence if:

(a) the action was unavoidable

(b) it was not possible for the seals to be replaced by an approved fitter or workshop

(c) the equipment in all other respects was being used in accordance with the regulations.

Reminders

The centre field of the chart must be completed **before** placing it in the instrument and again when finishing the working day or when a change of vehicles takes place.

If working away from the vehicle for any length of time the driver should make sure that the mode selector is correctly positioned for recording the working time; alternatively, he should take the chart with him and enter the details by hand (this is especially important if the vehicle is left standing for any period, ie in the yard where someone else could drive it). The driver may also be taking a statutory break during this period which must be recorded.

Drivers should remember to operate the mode selector switch so that it is recording the work actually being performed at any given time (see page 53).

The chart can be left in the vehicle for up to 24 hours but it is not advisable to do this unless it is certain that the vehicle will not be moved during the driver's absence, or that he will return before the chart overruns.

Drivers should note that the chart is a personal record of the hours they have worked; it is not a log for the vehicle.

Individual record books

If a driver is exempt from the tachograph regulations but is required to keep records in accordance with British law, he has the option of using either the tachograph or the individual record book.

If the record book is used it must be of A6 format (105mm x 148mm) or larger, and consist of a front sheet; instructions to the driver on how to complete the records; guidance notes for the employer, driver or owner driver; and weekly record sheets, in duplicate complete with carbon paper or some other means which allows duplicates to be made simultaneously.

The front sheet must contain the following information —
1. Date book first used.
2. Date book last used.
3. Surname, first name and address of the holder of the book.
4. Name, address, telephone number and stamp (if any) of the employer.
5. Name, address, telephone number and stamp (if any) of any other employer.
6. Operator's Licence No.

The operator must complete items 4 and 6 before issuing the book to the driver.

The driver has to enter his name and address at item 3 (an owner driver need not use item 3 unless his personal address is different to his business address) and date book is first used.

After all the weekly sheets have been used the date inserted at item 2. If the driver ceases to be employed by the employer who issued the book the date at item 2 is the last date of employment.

A new sheet must be used each week. A week is from midnight Sunday/Monday to midnight the next Sunday/Monday.

The driver must complete boxes 1 and 2 of the sheet at the start of the week and thereafter, on every day that is relevant, boxes 3-9 at the appropriate times.

All entries must be made in ink or with a ball-point pen. No erasures may be made and any corrections required must be made in such a way so as not to obliterate the original entry. Corrections must be initialled.

More than one employer
Where a driver has more than one employer the first employer is responsible for issuing the record book. The driver must, if requested, produce his record book for inspection by his employers.

Care and handling of record books
The book is personal to the driver and he must carry it with him whilst on duty and make it available to any authorised inspecting officer on request.

The driver must return the book within **7 days** of the end of each week of driving (or earlier if required) so that the employer can check and countersign the entries. The top sheet must be kept in the book and the duplicates removed and filed.

When all the weekly record sheets have been used the driver must keep the record book for **fourteen days** from the date the book is returned to him before he is next on duty by his employer — at the end of this period it must be returned to his employer who must preserve it, together with the duplicate sheets for at least twelve months.

Inspection and enforcement

The employer has the right to inspect his drivers' record books at any time.

Department of Transport enforcement staff and the police have the right to detain a vehicle for as long as is necessary to examine or copy information from the records to ensure that the drivers' hours regulations are being complied with.

Exemptions

A driver is exempt from having to keep records if he drives a vehicle not exceeding 3.5 tonnes maximum gross weight. Also, drivers operating under the **British domestic rules** need not keep records if they drive for no more than four hours on any day of the week *and* do not go outside a 50km radius from the operating base.

Note: whilst record keeping is not required in these circumstances, an employer has the right to ask the driver to keep some form of record to comply with company requirements.

DRINK AND DRIVING

Under the provisions of the Road Traffic Act 1988 it is an offence to drive, attempt to drive or be in charge of a motor vehicle, when having consumed alcohol in such quantity that the proportion of breath alcohol concentration exceeds the prescribed limit, ie 35 microgrammes of alcohol in 100 mililitres of breath (which is equivalent to 80 milligrammes of alcohol in 100 millilitres of blood or 107 milligrammes of alcohol in 100 millilitres of urine).

Penalties prescribed are, on summary conviction, a fine not exceeding £2000, or imprisonment for up to six months, or both.

On conviction on indictment a fine or imprisonment of up to two years, or both, can be imposed; (the maximum period of imprisonment on indictment for being in charge of a motor vehicle is one year). In addition, licence disqualification is usually imposed.

Breath tests and laboratory tests

A constable in uniform can require a driver to take a breath test at the road side if:

(a) he has reasonable cause to suspect the driver of having alcohol in his body

(b) he has reasonable cause to suspect the driver of having committed a moving traffic offence

(c) the driver has been involved in an accident.

Failure to take the test, without reasonable cause, renders him liable to arrest and prosecution.

If a preliminary test indicates that the driver is over the limit he will be required to go to the police station and unless he goes voluntarily he can be arrested without a warrant.

At the police station the driver may be required to provide two samples of breath for analysis by an electronic breath testing machine (which gives an instant print out of breath alchohol concentrations) or a specimen of blood or urine for laboratory tests.

Failure, without reasonable cause, to provide a specimen of breath, blood or urine renders him liable to prosecution and the constable must warn him of this at the time he asks for a specimen.

A statement automatically produced by the breath testing machine and a certificate signed by the police constable that the statement relates to the breath specimen supplied, and blood and urine specimens, shall be admissable as evidence in a prosecution.

A blood specimen may only be taken by a medical practitioner with the driver's consent.

Of any two breath specimens provided the lower must be used, except if the lower specimen shows no more than 50 microgrammes of alcohol in 100 millilitres of breath the driver has the right to replace the breath test with a blood or urine test.

Detention at the police station until the breath test indicates that the alcohol level is below the prescribed limit is possible.

There is a statutory defence against being "in charge" of a motor vehicle if a driver can prove that, at the time, circumstances were such that there was no likelihood of him driving whilst he exceeded the prescribed limits or whilst he was unfit through drugs.

Where there has been an accident involving injury to a third party, the police have the power to enter any place where a drink/drive suspect may be, using force if necessary, both to breathalyse and arrest him.

DRIVING OFFENCES AND DISQUALIFICATION

Disqualification
There are offences for which:

(a) endorsement is compulsory unless there are special reasons

(b) courts have discretionary powers to disqualify

(c) if **12** penalty points are accumulated over three years, disqualification will result for at least six months. Once a period of disqualification has been imposed the licence is "wiped clean" and those points do not count again.

Where more than one offence is committed on the same occasion the highest number of points for one offence will be awarded.

The three year period is a rolling term, ie it is measured on each occasion from the date the latest offence was committed.

When the disqualification is imposed after the total number of points have been awarded the period of disqualification will be:

— *six months*, if there has been no previous disqualification within the three years

— *one year*, if there has been one previous disqualification within the three years

— *two years*, if there has been more than one disqualification within the three years.

Disqualification can still be imposed for a single offence if it is considered to be serious enough and the liability to obligatory disqualification is retained for drinking and driving offences. (Drivers disqualified on conviction for drunken driving are subject to a minimum ban of one year for a first offence and three years for a second conviction for drunken driving within 10 years.)

Offences for which penalty points are awarded

Courts disqualifying a driver for any of the specified offences may order him to undergo another driving test prior to the reissue of his licence.

Offence	*No. of points*
Use of special road contrary to scheme or regulations	3
Contravention of pedestrian crossing regulations	3
Not stopping at school crossing	3
Contravention of order relating to street playground	2
Exceeding speed limit	3
Causing death by reckless driving	(a)
Reckless driving	(b)
Careless and inconsiderate driving	3-9
Driving or attempting to drive when unfit to drive through drink or drugs	(a)

Being in charge of a vehicle when unfit to drive through drink or drugs	10
Driving or attempting to drive with excess alcohol in body	(a)
Being in charge of a vehicle with excess alcohol in body	10
Failing to provide a specimen for breath test	4
Failing to provide specimen for analysis or laboratory test	(a)
Motor racing and speed trials on public ways	(b)
Leaving vehicle in dangerous position	3
Failing to comply with traffic directions	3
Failing to comply with traffic signs	3
Contravention of construction and use regulations	3
Driving without a licence	2
Driving with uncorrected eyesight, or refusing a test of eyesight	2
Failing to comply with conditions attached to a provisional or full licence	2
Driving while disqualified—	
where offender was disqualified as under age	2
where offender was disqualified by order of court	6
Using motor vehicle without insurance	6-8
Failing to stop after accident and give particulars or report accident	8-10
Taking, etc, vehicle without consent, driving it or allowing oneself to be carried in it	8
Manslaughter or, in Scotland, culpable homicide	(a)
Stealing or attempting to steal a motor vehicle	8
Going equipped for stealing, etc., motor vehicles	8

(a) 4 points if under exceptional circumstances disqualification is not imposed.
(b) 4, or 10 points, depending on circumstances, if disqualification is not imposed.

Schedule of Offences

The Criminal Justice Act 1982 introduced a scale of fines for summary offences known as the "standard scale" which sets the levels of maximum fines, depending on the severity of the offence. There are five levels and the maximum amounts of each level are currently:

Level 1	£50
Level 2	£100
Level 3	£400
Level 4	£1,000
Level 5	£2,000

The Road Traffic Offenders Act 1988 lists the offences and levels applicable. Offences relating to the use of motor vehicles, etc. are detailed as follows (offences marked with an asterisk also include endorsement of the driving licence with penalty points if the driver is not disqualified).

Offence	Level and/or other penalty
Contravention of traffic regulation order ...	3
Contravention of order regulating traffic in Greater London	3
Contravention of experimental traffic order	3
Contravention of experimental traffic scheme in Greater London	3
Contravention of temporary prohibition or restriction	3
Use of special road contrary to scheme or regulations	4*
One-way traffic on trunk road	3
Contravention of prohibition or restriction of roads of certain classes	3
Contravention of pedestrian crossing regulations	3*
Not stopping at school crossing	3*
Contravention of order relating to school playground	3*

Contravention of order relating to use of parking space	3
Unauthorised use of loading area	3
Contravention of minimum speed limit	3
Exceeding speed limit	3*
Interference with immobilisation device	3
Ignoring excess charge notice	3
False response to excess charge notice	5
Failure to give information as to identity of driver	3
Failure to give evidence at an enquiry	3
Causing death by reckless driving	*On indictment — 5 years
Reckless driving	*Summarily — 6 months
Careless and inconsiderate driving	4*
Driving or attempting to drive when unfit through drink or drugs	5* and/or 6 months
Being in charge of a vehicle when unfit to drive through drink or drugs	4* and/or 3 months
Driving or attempting to drive with excess alcohol in body	5* and/or 6 months
Being in charge of vehicle with excess alcohol in body	4* and/or 3 months
Failing to provide a breath specimen for test	3*
Failing to provide specimen for analysis or lab. test to ascertain ability to drive, etc.	5* and/or 6 months
Motor racing and speed trials on public ways	4*
Other unauthorised competitions or trials on public ways	3
Driving or riding in a vehicle without wearing a seat belt	2
Driving vehicle with child in front not wearing seat belt	2
Parking heavy commercial vehicles on verges, etc.	3
Driving or parking on cycle tracks	3
Leaving vehicle in dangerous position	3*
Tampering with motor vehicles	3

Driving motor vehicles elsewhere than on roads...	3
Failing to comply with traffic directions.......	3*
Failing to comply with traffic signs.............	3*
Contravention of construction and use regulations	
— using, or causing or permitting the use of a goods vehicle in a dangerous condition or because of weight, distribution..	5*
packing or adjustment of its load etc. ...	
— using a vehicle with an insecure load....	5*
— in any other case	4*
Using vehicle without current test certificate	
— adapted to carry more than 8 passengers	4
— in any other case	3
Driver of goods vehicle not in attendance while vehicle being tested......................	3
Using, etc., goods vehicle without current plating certificate	3
Using, etc., goods vehicle without current test certificate	3
Using, etc., goods vehicle which has been altered and not notified to Sec. of State as required by RTA '88 s.49.....................	3
Driver of goods vehicle not in attendance whilst vehicle being tested following alteration	3
Using, etc., goods vehicle without type approval certificate	4
Using, etc., certain goods vehicles for drawing trailers when plating certificate does not specify maximum laden weights	3
Using, etc., goods vehicle which has been altered but not notified to Sec. of State in relation to certificate of conformity or Minister's approval certificate	3
Using goods vehicles with unauthorised as well as authorised weights marked on it....	3

Supplying vehicle or vehicle parts without appropriate type approval certificate being in force............................ 5

Obstructing vehicle examiner from testing vehicle on road to ascertain its roadworthiness, etc. 3

Obstructing inspection of goods vehicle by examiner or failing to comply with requirement to take vehicle for inspection . 3

Driving a goods vehicle in contravention of a prohibition or failing to comply with direction to remove an overloaded vehicle 5

Failing to inspect, and keep records of inspections of, goods vehicles............... 3

Selling, etc., unroadworthy vehicle or trailer or altering same to make unroadworthy ... 5

Fitting of defective or unsuitable vehicle parts 5

Supplying defective or unsuitable vehicle parts 4

Obstructing examiner from testing vehicles to ascertain if defective or unsuitable parts have been fitted 3

Obstructing examiner from testing condition of used vehicles at salerooms, etc. 3

Failing to comply with requirements about weighing motor vehicle or obstructing authorised person 5

Driving without a licence 3*

Causing or permitting a person to drive without a licence.............................. 3

Failure to notify DVLC of onset of, or worsening of relevant or prospective disability.. 3

Driving with defective eyesight, or refusing to have eyesight test 3*

Failing to comply with the conditions relating to provisional licence...................... 3*

Failing to comply with any conditions prescribed for driving under provisional

licence where conditions are applicable to full licence	3*
Failure to advise change of particulars on licence	3
Obtaining driving licence while disqualified..	3
Driving while disqualified	5* and/or 6 months (in Scotland 6 months or the statutory maximum)
Failing to produce to court N. Ireland driving licence	3
Driving or permitting the driving of HGV without HGV licence	4
Failing to comply with any conditions of HGV licence, or permitting person under 21 to drive HGV in contravention of such conditions......................................	3
Using motor vehicle without insurance	4*
Failing to surrender insurance certificate on cancellation or to make statutory declaration of loss or destruction	3
Failing to give information or making false statement when making an insurance claim	4
Failing to stop when required by constable...	3
Failing to produce driving licence to constable or to state date of birth	3
Failing to give constable certain names and addresses or to produce certain documents	3
Refusing to give, or giving false name and address in case of reckless or inconsiderate driving..	3
Failing to stop after accident and give particulars or report accident	5*
Failure by driver, in case of accident involving injury to another to produce evidence of insurance or to report accident	3

Failure by owner of vehicle to give information to police concerning compulsory insurance	4
Failure of person keeping vehicle and others to give police information as to the identity of driver, etc.	3
Forgery, etc., of licences, test certificates, insurance certificates and other documents	Statutory maximum
Making certain false statements and withholding certain material information	4
Issuing false documents	4
Impersonation of authorised examiner	3
Taking, etc., in Scotland, a vehicle without the owner's consent, driving it or allowing oneself to be carried in it	3 months and/or statutory maximum*
Failing to attend, give evidence or produce documents to enquiry held by Secretary of State	3
Obstructing inspection of vehicles after accident	3
Failing to give date of birth or sex to court, etc.	3
Failing to produce driving licence to court for interim disqualification on committal for sentence, etc.	3
Failing to produce licence to court for endorsement, etc	3
Applying for or obtaining a licence without giving particulars of current endorsement .	3
Removing fixed penalty notice from vehicle .	2
False statement in response to notice to owner	5

These penalties apply to first convictions only; subsequent convictions incur heavier penalties.

Note: the police have powers to seize an offender's driving licence when the offence involves obligatory endorsement if he fails to deliver it to the court.

Removal of disqualification

If a person has been disqualified he may apply to the clerk of the court which disqualified him for the removal of the disqualification under the following conditions:

(a) if the disqualification is for less than four years, when two years from the date on which it was imposed have expired

(b) if the disqualification is for less than 10 years, but not less than four years, when half the period of disqualification has expired

(c) in any other case, when five years have expired from the date of disqualification.

If the first removal application is refused, others can be made at three month intervals.

If disqualification is for two years or less application for the removal of the disqualification cannot be made. However, application to the quarter sessions for a reduction of the period can be made within 14 days of conviction and disqualification.

Courts disqualifying a driver from driving for any of the offences outlined in the above-mentioned schedules may order him to undergo another driving test prior to the reissue of his licence. A driving test cannot be ordered for any other road traffic offence.

If prosecuted for any of the offences listed, the driver must:

(a) submit his driving licence to the clerk of the court not later than the day before the hearing or

(b) post his licence to the court to be received not later than the day of the hearing or

(c) take his licence to the hearing.

Removal of endorsements

Endorsements are not removed from a driving licence until four years after conviction; for drinking and other driving offences the endorsements remain for 11 years.

Dual liability

In respect of the under-mentioned offences both the driver or owner-driver and the employer are involved.

1. Contravention of an order relating to street playgrounds.
2. Contravention of construction and use regulations:
   (a) in a manner likely to cause danger — vehicle over-weight, insecure load, etc
   (b) by breach of requirements as to brakes, steering gear, tyres
   (c) by driving whilst unqualified and employing and allowing a person who does not hold a licence to drive the type of motor vehicle in question
   (d) by the use of a motor vehicle uninsured or unsecured against third party risks.

An employer who permits or causes the vehicle to be used can also be prosecuted. A defence can be made if the employer can prove that he did not know that the offence had been committed.

DOCUMENTATION

The documentary procedures with which a driver is concerned in his daily duties are quite formidable. It is for this reason that a list of the required information with the necessary documents is given below for ready reference.

Most of this information should be issued by the employer, but a certain amount still remains the responsibility of the driver. In the case of owner-drivers there is a dual responsibility.

To simplify the procedure the information and documents required to support the driver in the efficient and speedy progress of his professional duties, are listed under the following headings — *Operation, Service, Safety*.

Some of the information should be affixed to the vehicle, ie maximum vehicle gross weight, tyre pressures, current excise licence disc, operator's licence disc. In the case of the last two items it is also the duty of the driver to see that they are always displayed in the cab of the vehicle.

Operation
1. Driving licence (ordinary and HGV/LGV if applicable).
2. Accident insurance form.
3. Name, address and telephone number of headquarters, base, branch or depot.
4. Tachograph charts (records of driving, rest periods and breaks).
5. Operator's licence number.
6. Vehicle registration number.
7. Schedule and route of deliveries.

Service
1. Maximum gross vehicle weight and pay load.
2. Consignment, collection and delivery notes.
3. Bridge clearance limits en route and vehicle load or body height. The latter is a statutory requirement if the vehicle and load **exceeds** 3.66m (12 feet) in overall height and a notice showing the height must be displayed in the cab (see page 92).

Safety
1. Tyres — pressures, size and make.
2. Fuel — supply point and agency card arrangements.
3. Repairs — names and telephone number of firms appointed for immediate contact.
4. Tremcard — if carrying dangerous substances (see pages 191 and 195).

Employers should supply a suitable wallet in which to hold such information; some information may, of course, be posted in the cab. Whichever method is used the information must be readily available to the driver to enable him to act promptly in any emergency.

Communication
Transport and distribution operations demand the best possible communication services and therefore the documentation and information referred to throughout this

book provide a most necessary means of supporting such communications. If a driver is stopped by the police or Department of Transport officials in connection with the inspection of a vehicle, its load, breakdown or accident, he will have the means of communicating promptly with the respective services and his employer, to ensure that the occurrence is acted upon with the minimum delay.

SPEED LIMITS

The maximum speed on motorways and other dual carriageway roads is 70 mph and on single carriageway roads 60 mph unless lower speeds are in force, ie on restricted roads the limit is usually 30 mph.

Speed limits apply to roads and vehicles where these are different the lowest speed limit applies.

The following speed limits apply to the various classes of vehicle:

Class of Vehicle	Motor-ways	Dual carriage-ways	Other roads
Private cars, car-derived vans†, or dual-purpose vehicles not adapted to carry more than eight passengers	70	70*	60*
Private cars, car-derived vans†, or dual-purpose vehicles drawing one trailer	60	60*	50*
Rigid goods vehicles not exceeding 7.5 tonnes gross vehicle weight and not drawing a trailer	70	60*	50*
Articulated vehicles not exceeding 7.5 tonnes gross train weight, goods vehicles (not being car-derived vans) drawing one trailer where the total laden weight of the vehicle and trailer does not exceed 7.5 tonnes.	60	60*	50*

* provided the particular roads are not subject to lower limits.
† a "car-derived van" is a goods vehicle constructed or adapted as a derivative of a passenger vehicle not exceeding 2 tonnes maximum laden weight.

Class of Vehicle	Motor-ways	Dual carriage-ways	Other roads
Articulated vehicles exceeding 7.5 tonnes gross train weight, goods vehicles exceeding 7.5 tonnes gross vehicle weight without trailer, or when drawing a trailer the total weight of the vehicle and trailer exceeds 7.5 tonnes gross weight.	60	50*	40*
Goods vehicle drawing more than one trailer.	40	20	20
Passenger vehicles having an unladen weight exceeding 3.05 tonnes or adapted to carry more than eight passengers:			
(a) not exceeding 12m in overall length	70	60*	50*
(b) exceeding 12m in overall length	60	60*	50*
Motor tractor (other than an industrial tractor), light locomotive or heavy locomotive:			
(a) provided it is equipped with suitable and sufficient springs between wheels and frame and, unless the body affords protection, it is fitted with wings, etc (if drawing a trailer to which the foregoing provisions also apply)	40	30	30
(b) in any other case	20	20	20

*provided the particular roads are not subject to lower limits.

Class of Vehicle	Motor-ways	Dual carriage-ways	Other roads
Works truck	18	18	18
Industrial tractor	n/a	18	18
Agricultural vehicle	40	40	40*
Vehicles operating under the "Special Types" categories are subject to the following limits:			
Category 1	60	50*	40*
Category 2	40	35	30
Category 3	30	25	20
Vehicles carrying wide loads exceeding 4.3m up to 6.1m	30	25	20

For detailed information on driving on motorways see page 152.

*provided the particular roads are not subject to lower limits

PEDESTRIAN CROSSINGS AND BUS LANES

Zebra crossings

Zebra crossings consist of rows of alternate black and white stripes between two rows of round or square-headed metal studs placed across the road and marked by a yellow globe on a post containing a flashing light (Belisha beacons). In certain circumstances a constant light may be used.

On either the approach side or both sides of the zebra crossing (depending on local requirements), there is a "zebra controlled area" consisting of two or more white broken zig-zag lines, starting from short lines across the road and approaching the crossing, finishing at a dotted line, the give way line, 1m before reaching the row of metal studs edging the actual zebra crossing.

In the zebra controlled area **overtaking is prohibited and vehicles must stop at the give way line**.

Stopping in the controlled area or on the crossing is also prohibited except to allow pedestrians to cross, or in circumstances beyond the driver's control.

Pedestrians must be given the right of way if they are already on a crossing before a vehicle reaches it. On roads divided by a central reservation or a street refuge (island), each half of the road is treated as a separate crossing.

Pelican crossings
Pelican crossings are controlled by lights and are operated by pedestrians. The difference between conventional three-light signals and the Pelican signals is the flashing amber signal which appears immediately after the red as opposed to the red/ amber signal. Pedestrians continue to have precedence on a crossing when the amber light is flashing but if no pedestrians are crossing vehicles may proceed.

Bus lanes
Bus lanes on general purpose roads are reserved for public service vehicles only and it is an offence for other vehicles to enter these lanes when they are in operation (usually during peak hours). The lanes are clearly marked with special signs indicating times of operation.

Road traffic signs
A booklet entitled *Know Your Traffic Signs*, is available from HMSO and gives detailed information on the complete range of signs and road markings, including full explanations of waiting restrictions and direction signs.

THE VEHICLE

BRAKES

The law lays down specific requirements as to the design, application and maintenance of brakes.

Every goods vehicle must be equipped with either an efficient braking system with two means of operation, or two efficient braking systems having separate means of operation.

Parking brakes

Every motor vehicle must have a braking system to prevent at least two wheels (one if a three-wheeler) revolving when the vehicle is not being driven. All vehicles registered after 1.1.68, must have an independent parking brake. The parking brake by direct mechanical action must be capable of holding the vehicle stationary on a gradient of at least 16% (ie 1 in 6.25).

Braking efficiency

Goods vehicles having at least four wheels and required to have two means of operating brakes must have braking efficiencies as follows:

Registered before 1.1.68
Rigid vehicle (with two axles)
First means 45%
Second means 20%
Rigid vehicle (with more than two axles)
First means 45%
Second means 15%

Registered on or after 1.1.68
First means 50%
Second means 25%

Vehicles and trailers first used on and after 1.4.83, must be fitted with a braking system which complies with certain EC directives. These lay down technical standards on braking and stopping stability and downhill speed control of vehicles.

The parking brake of motor vehicles must be capable of holding the vehicle and any trailer attached stationary on a gradient of 12% (1 in 8.33).

DIRECTION INDICATORS

All vehicles must be fitted with direction indicators. Indicators can be of the flashing or semaphore type but the latter may only be fitted to vehicles registered before September 1965. Indicators on vehicles first used from September 1965 must show amber both to the front and rear.

GLASS

Windscreens and windows should be kept clean to ensure a clear view of the road and other traffic.

HORNS

Every motor vehicle must be fitted with an instrument, capable of giving audible and sufficient warning of its approach or position. A horn fitted to a motor vehicle must not be sounded when the vehicle is stationary on the road or when in motion on a restricted road (where the street lamps are not more than 200 yards apart) between 23.30 hours and 07.00 hours except in an emergency.

REVERSING ALARMS

These may be fitted to goods vehicles having a maximum gross weight of 2 tonnes or more, engineering plant and works trucks. The sound emitted by the reversing alarm must be different to that which is employed at "pelican" pedestrian crossings so that no confusion is caused.

Reversing alarms may not be sounded between 23.30 hours and 07.00 hours on a restricted road.

SIDEGUARDS

Most goods vehicles exceeding 3.5 tonnes gross vehicle weight first used from 1.4.84 and trailers and semi-trailers exceeding 1020kg unladen weight manufactured from 1.5.83 need to be fitted with sideguards. However, in the case of semi-trailers manufactured **before** 1.5.83 sideguards are only required if (a) the semi-trailer has a plated gross weight exceeding 26,000kg, (b) the distance between the centre of the first axle and the centre of the kingpin (the rearmost one if there is more than one) exceeds 4.5m and (c) the plated train weight of the tractive unit **exceeds** 32,520kg.

If the semi-trailer was made **before** 1.5.83 and is attached to a tractive unit having a plated train weight not exceeding 32,520kg, sideguards are not required.

Where the company employs a mixture of semi-trailers with and without sideguards and tractive units above and below 32,520kg gross train weight, care must be taken when coupling the two together to ensure that, so far as the sideguards law is concerned, they are legal for use on the road.

SPRAY SUPPRESSION EQUIPMENT

Spray suppression equipment conforming to British Standard Specifications has to be fitted in relation to the wheels of each axle of goods vehicles exceeding 12 tonnes maximum gross weight first used from 1.4.86 and trailers exceeding 3.5 tonnes maximum gross weight manufactured from 1.5.85. Trailers exceeding 16 tonnes maximum gross weight having two or more axles manufactured before 1.5.85 had to be fitted with this equipment by 1.10.87.

LIGHTING

During the hours of darkness all vehicles are required to carry two lamps showing white to the front, two lamps showing red to the rear, two red reflectors also to the rear and, in most cases, two headlamps.

Restrictions
1. **A red light must not** be shown to the front of a vehicle.
2. **A white light must not** be shown to the rear of a vehicle except in the following circumstances:
   (a) for the purpose of reversing
   (b) in order to illuminate the interior of a vehicle
   (c) to illuminate the rear number plate

(d) to illuminate a public service vehicle destination board and a taxi meter.

Special provisions do permit the use of blue, amber or green lights on fire, ambulance, police service vehicles, medical practitioner's vehicles, and special service vehicles.

Use of front position lamps

Front position lamps and rear position lamps must be switched on when a vehicle is being driven on the road between **sunset** and **sunrise.**

Use of headlamps and auxiliary lamps

Headlamps must be used during the **hours of darkness** in all unlit areas (or where the street lamps are more than 200 yards apart). "Hours of darkness" is usually defined as half an hour after sunset to half an hour before sunrise.

Both lights must be illuminated together and it is an offence to drive with only one headlamp working.

Headlamps must be switched off when the vehicle is stationary except at traffic stops. They must not be fitted more than 1200mm from the ground (except on engineering plant), nor less than 500mm from the ground.

Headlamps must be fitted with a dipping mechanism to avoid dazzle and no light other than a dipping headlight may be moved, by swivelling or otherwise, while the vehicle is in motion. Every matched pair of headlamps must emit beams of the same colour light. In the case of lamps fitted and used as fog or spotlights, these must be fitted with a permanently deflected beam. There is no minimum height for these lamps provided they are used only during poor visibility.

Road clearance vehicles are permitted to use only one headlamp. A vehicle being towed and a snow plough are exempt from using headlamps.

Front fog lamps

In conditions where visibility is seriously reduced, two fog lamps or a fog lamp and a spot lamp may be used instead of headlamps.

Fog lamps may emit either a white or yellow light and must be positioned so that they do not dazzle or cause inconvenience to other road users.

Rear fog lamps

Rear fog lamps must be fitted to vehicles and trailers first used from 1.4.80. Either a single or a matched pair of rear fog lamps can be fitted.

Rear fog lamps may only be used in conditions of poor visibility and must be switched *off* as soon as conditions improve.

End outline marker lamps

Motor vehicles first used from 1.4.91 and trailers manufactured from 1.10.90 must be fitted with at least two outline marker lamps at the front of the vehicle or trailer and at least two at the rear in matched pairs.

The lamps must be switched on when the vehicle is used on the road between sunset and sunrise and also during daylight hours when visibility is seriously reduced.

Side marker lamps

Side marker lamps must be fitted to certain vehicles or combinations of vehicles, depending on length and these lamps must be lit when such vehicles are used on the road at *night*, or during *daylight* hours when visibility is *seriously reduced*.

Lamps required

1. A vehicle or a combination of vehicles (including any load) being more than **18.3m** in overall length:

   (a) one lamp, no part of the light emitting surface being more than **9.15m** from the front of the vehicle, inclusive of loads

   (b) one lamp, no part of the light emitting surface being more than **3.05m** from the rear of the vehicle, or vehicles, inclusive of load

   (c) other lamps as required so that the distance between any part of their light emitting surfaces are not more than **3.05m** apart.

2. A combination of vehicles the overall length (including any load) being more than **12.2m** but not more than **18.3m** and carrying a load supported by any two of the vehicles but not including a load carried by an articulated vehicle:

    (a) one lamp, no part of its light emitting surface being forward of, or more than **1530mm** rearward of, the rearmost part of the drawing vehicle

    (b) if the supported load extends more than **9.15m** rearward of the rearmost part of the drawing vehicle, one lamp is required, the light emitting surface being within **1530mm** of the centre point of the length of load.

3. Any trailer (not covered by 1 or 2 above) exceeding **9.15m** in overall length (excluding any drawbar or fitting attachment): one lamp required on each side, the light emitting surface being within **1530mm** of the centre point of the overall length of the trailer.

Side marker lamps must show a white light to the front and a red light to the rear.

Motor vehicles first used from 1.4.91 and trailers manufactured from 1.10.90 in either case being more than 6m in overall length (excluding the drawbar on the trailer) must be fitted with side marker lamps at 3m intervals on each side.

Lighting on projecting trailers and overhanging or projecting loads or equipment on vehicles

Trailers forming part of a combination of vehicles and which are wider than any preceding vehicle and the loads being carried on any vehicle which are wider than the vehicle, must carry lamps outlining their width in the following circumstances.

1. If a trailer, not fitted with front position lamps, is wider on any side than the preceding vehicle, to the extent that the outermost part of the illuminated area of the obligatory front position lamp fitted to any preceding vehicle is more than **400mm**, a lamp showing a white light to the front must be fitted to the trailer with the outermost illuminated area

of the light being not more than **400mm** from the outermost edge of the trailer.

2. If a trailer carries a load which is wider than the trailer and the preceding vehicle, and the circumstances are similar to 1 above, a lamp showing a white light to the front must be fitted to the trailer, or load, or equipment so that the outermost part of the illuminating area of the lamp is not more than **400mm** from the outer edge of the load or equipment, etc.

3. If a vehicle carries a load which is wider on any side of the vehicle so that the distance from the edge of the load or equipment, to the outermost edge of the illuminated area of the obligatory front or rear position lamp on that side exceeds **400mm**, then either (a) the front or rear position lamp must be transferred to the load, etc or (b) an additional front or rear position lamp must be fitted to the vehicle, load or equipment. Installation, performance and maintenance requirements of the lamps must be complied with except that so far as lateral positioning is concerned, reference to the vehicle shall also include the load or equipment but not special equipment such as movable platform or a crane jib on the vehicle.

4. If a vehicle carries a load or equipment which projects beyond the rear of the vehicle, or rearmost vehicle if more than one, by more than (a) **2m** if an agricultural vehicle or a vehicle carrying a fire escape, or (b) **1m** in any other case, an additional red rear light must be fitted to the vehicle or load within **2m** of the rearmost part of the load in the case of (a) or **1m** in the case of (b) above.

5. If a vehicle carries a load which obscures any obligatory lamp, reflector or rear marking steps must be taken to either (a) transfer the obligatory lamp, rear reflector or rear marking to the load, or (b) attach an additional lamp, reflector or rear marking to the vehicle or load.

Where it is necessary for these lamps, reflectors or rear markings to be fitted, their performance and/or maintenance must comply with the requirements of the regulations.

Lamps must be lit at night and during the day if visibility is seriously reduced.

Emergency and other services' vehicles

Distinctive lamps emitting blue, amber or green flashing lights are permitted on certain vehicles carrying out emergency or other services.

Ambulances, fire engines, fire salvage vehicles, Forestry Commission or local authority vehicles used for fire fighting, police vehicles, blood transfusion service vehicles, bomb disposal, RAF mountain rescue vehicles, HM coastguard or coastguard auxiliary vehicles used for emergencies on or near the coast, NCB mine rescue vehicles, RNLI vehicles used for launching lifeboats and vehicles used for carrying human tissue for transplants, etc, are permitted to carry one or more **blue** lamps.

Vehicles used for road clearance; for testing, maintaining, improving, cleansing or watering roads; inspecting, renewing or installing any apparatus in, on, under or over a road; vehicles constructed or adapted for refuse collection; vehicles having a maximum speed not exceeding 25 mph; vehicles having an overall width exceeding 2.9m; breakdown vehicles; vehicles authorised by an Order under s.44 of the Road Traffic Act 1988, ie Special Type vehicles or trailers constructed for special purposes, etc and vehicles used by HM Customs & Excise for testing fuels, are permitted to carry one or more **amber** lights.

Vehicles used by registered medical practitioners registered by the General Medical Council may carry one or more **green** lamps when used in an emergency.

Warning beacons fitted to vehicles used at airports may emit a **yellow** light.

All such lamps must be fitted so that the centre is at least **1200mm** above the ground and be visible from any point at a reasonable distance from the vehicle. The frequency of the flashing from these lamps must not be less than 60 nor more than 240 equal times per minute and the interval between each flashing must be constant.

The lamps may only be used when the vehicle is being used for the relevant purposes and in the case of a breakdown vehicle the amber lights may only be illuminated when the vehicle is being used in connection with, or near to, an accident or breakdown, or towing a disabled vehicle. Such vehicles are permitted an additional white lamp for illuminating the area of the accident or breakdown but it must be directed so as not to dazzle or inconvenience other road users.

Road clearance vehicles are also permitted to carry an amber reflecting surface to the rear of the vehicle.

Obligatory warning beacons

Motor vehicles with four or more wheels having a maximum speed not exceeding 25 mph and any trailer drawn by such a vehicle, when used on an unrestricted dual carriageway road, ie, where the permitted legal speed limit is over 50 mph, must be fitted with at least one amber warning beacon **which must be lit.**

This requirement does not apply to a vehicle or trailer being towed if it is crossing the road in the quickest manner possible.

The lamp or lamps must be fitted so that their centres are at least 1200mm above the ground and be visible from any point at a reasonable distance from the vehicle which means that where a motor vehicle is towing a trailer and the load on the trailer obscures the lamp on the drawing vehicle steps must be taken to either move the lamp or fit an extra lamp to the trailer so that the regulations are complied with.

Stop lights, reversing and parking lights

Stop lights must be fitted to all vehicles and must always be maintained in a clean and efficient working order.

Reversing and parking lights are not compulsory fittings but if fitted to a vehicle they must be maintained in efficient working order. See page 169 for parking vehicles without lights.

Trailer and trailer caravan lighting requirements are the same as those applying to motor vehicles with few exceptions. Trailers which do not have side lamps *must* have front corner lamps.

Hazard warning lights

Hazard warning lights may be used only when the vehicle is stationary on any part of the road, for the purpose of warning other drivers that the vehicle is temporarily causing an obstruction or when on a motorway or unrestricted dual-carriageway to warn following drivers to slow down owing to an obstruction ahead.

Lights required during daylight hours

The law requires vehicles travelling on a road where visibility is seriously reduced to have obligatory lamps switched on, ie front side, end outline marker lamps (where fitted) and rear position lamps and either headlamps, or a pair of front fog lamps and rear fog lamps. For large goods vehicles and trailers side marker lamps are also required to be lit.

It should be noted that front and rear fog lamps may *only* be used in conditions where visibility is *seriously reduced* during the day or at night — it is illegal to use them at any other time.

General requirements

Headlamps, front and rear fog lamps and reversing lamps (if fitted) must be set so that they do not dazzle or cause incon-venience to other road users. It is also a requirement of the law that all obligatory lights and reflectors, including hazard warn-ing lights are kept clean and in good working order.

VEHICLE MARKINGS

Owner's name and address

Generally speaking vehicles do not have to show the name and address of the owner. Such information is, however, required on the under-mentioned vehicles.

1. Every kind of vehicle from which milk is sold or offered for sale.

2. Milk tankers, which must display the name and address of the consignor.

3. Every dealer in ice cream who, in a public place in England and Wales, sells ice cream from a vehicle.

4. Vehicles and mobile shops from which any food is sold or carried and from which business is carried on.

Markings should be applied in 1 inch letters on the nearside of the vehicle.

Weight

The unladen weight of the vehicle must be printed or plainly marked on the chassis or some conspicuous place on the nearside of commercial vehicles over 3 tons, however this is not required for a vehicle where a Ministry plate has been issued which shows its unladen weight.

In accordance with the plating regulations, vehicles must carry plates showing their permitted gross and axle weights. This information may additionally be displayed on the nearside of vehicles for the guidance of weighbridge attendants.

Overall height

Motor vehicles, including articulated vehicles, drawbar trailer combinations, vehicles carrying skips, containers or engineering equipment, and engineering plant which exceed 3.66m (12 feet) in overall height, must display a notice in a prominent position in the driving cab, giving the total overall height of the vehicle and load. The measurements must be given in feet and inches in figures at least 40mm tall.

Number plates

Vehicles not exceeding 3 tons unladen weight, first registered on or after 1.1.73 must be fitted with reflex-reflecting number plates. Only the background may be made of reflex-reflecting material and this must be white for the front plate and yellow for the back plate with letters and figures in black on both.

Tractive units of articulated vehicles should be fitted with reflex-reflecting number plates if used on the road without a semi-trailer.

Vehicles first registered before 1.1.73 may also be fitted with reflex-reflecting number plates as an alternative to the existing type.

A trailer (including a broken-down vehicle being towed) must have the registration number of the towing vehicle fitted on the rear of the vehicle on tow.

Other markings

Vehicles carrying dangerous substances in packages (depending on quantities—see page 195) must be fitted with two rectangular reflectorised orange coloured plates (400mm long×300mm high) with a black border not exceeding 15mm in width. One plate must be positioned at the front of the vehicle and the other at the rear.

Motor vehicles, ie those over 7.5 tonnes gross weight, must be fitted with rear markings (see page 94) which are conspicuous in the light of headlamps and show up well in poor weather conditions. This also applies to trailers over 3.5 tonnes gross weight.

For motor vehicles up to 13m in overall length and trailer combinations up to 11m in overall length the rear markings must be of diagonal stripes of red fluorescent and yellow reflective material as shown in Diagrams 1 or 2; where the construction of the vehicle or trailer makes the fitting of markings in Diagrams 1 or 2 impractical, markings as shown in Diagram 3 may be fitted.

Vehicles and trailer combinations exceeding 13m in overall length must be fitted with a rear marking having the words "LONG VEHICLE" in black lettering on a yellow reflective background with a red fluorescent border as shown in Diagrams 4 or 5.

Trailer combinations exceeding 11m but not over 13m may fit either type of marking.

Rear markings must comply with BS AU 152: 1970.

It is a requirement of the regulations that **all rear markings** must be maintained in a **clean** and **efficient** condition while the vehicle is in use on the road. Drivers should examine rear markings periodically to ensure that they are clearly visible to drivers in following vehicles — this particularly applies to vehicles used in quarries or on building sites etc, where mud and other debris is thrown up thus reducing the reflective qualities of the rear markings.

Size and type of rear markings for goods vehicles and trailers

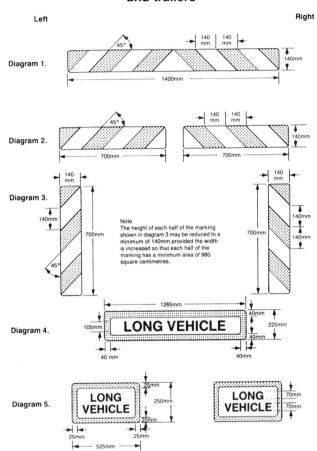

Left

Right

Diagram 1.

45°

140 mm | 140 mm

140mm

1400mm

Diagram 2.

45°

140 mm | 140 mm

140mm

700mm

700mm

Diagram 3.

140 mm

140mm

700mm

45°

Note
The height of each half of the marking shown in diagram 3 may be reduced to a minimum of 140mm provided the width is increased so that each half of the marking has a minimum area of 980 square centimetres.

140 mm

140mm

140mm

700mm

Diagram 4.

1265mm

40mm

105mm | LONG VEHICLE | 225mm

40mm

40 mm

40mm

Diagram 5.

LONG VEHICLE

25mm

250mm

25mm

LONG VEHICLE

70mm

70mm

25mm | 25mm

525mm

Size and type of markings for builders' skips

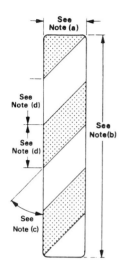 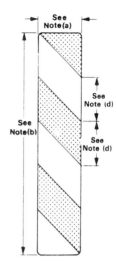

Notes:

(a) width — maximum 280mm; minimum 140mm

(b) length — maximum 700mm; minimum 350mm

(c) angle — maximum 50°; minimum 40° — to the vertical

(d) breadth — maximum 147mm; minimum 133mm.

The minimum area of each half of the marking must be at least 980 square centimetres.

The shaded area must be of red fluorescent material while the light area must be yellow reflective material.

Positioning

Markings must be securely fixed to the vehicle and must not project beyond the sides of the vehicle. The lower edge of each marking must be horizontal and not more than 1700mm nor less than 400mm from the ground. Where divided markings are used (Nos. 2, 3 and 5), the lower edges of each half must be level; each half must be the same distance from the centre and as near to the outermost edge of the vehicle as possible.

Markings as shown in diagrams 1 and 4 must be placed so that the centre of the markings is on the centre line of the vehicle.

If a load which projects to the rear of a vehicle obscures the rear marking an additional rear marking should be fitted to the end of the load.

The minimum area of each half of the marking must be at least 980 square centimetres.

The shaded area must be of red fluorescent material while the light area must be yellow reflective material.

Markings on builders' skips

Reflective markings are required to be fitted to builders' skips as shown on page 95. They must be fitted to each end of the skip when it is placed on any part of the highway (except a footpath or verge).

Two plates forming a pair are required at each end and they must be fitted (a) as near to the outer edge as possible on each side, but must not project beyond the edge of the skip; (b) they must be in a vertical position so that the innermost edge of each one is parallel to and the same distance from the vertical plane passing through the longitudinal axis of the skip; and (c) their upper edges must be parallel and not more than 1.5m from the ground and not lower than the upper edge of the skip depending on its construction. Neither plate should be fixed to any lid or door except when the door is the only convenient place for fixing.

Only plates bearing the BSI mark BS AU 1523: 1970 (and the marking in paragraph 5 of that Standard) may be fitted.

They must be kept clean and in good order and be clearly visible from a reasonable distance.

In addition to these requirements skips left on the highway at night must be marked with the name of the operator/owner and telephone number or address, and be kept lit.

Identification sign for "special types" vehicles
"Special types" vehicles ie vehicles and trailers used for hauling or carrying abnormal loads must be fitted with an identification sign. The sign must measure 400mm×250mm and show the following —

```
STGO
CAT
```

in white lettering on a black background. The letters on the first line must be 105mm high and on the second line (which must include the figure 1, 2 or 3 depending on the category of, or combination of vehicles) must be in letters 70mm high.

The sign must be mounted at the front of the vehicle, or vehicle combination.

Special types vehicles are subject to certain speed limits depending on category — see page 80.

MIRRORS

All goods vehicles and dual-purpose vehicles must have at least two mirrors, one fitted externally on the offside and the other either internally or externally on the nearside to show traffic to the rear and both sides rearwards.

On all vehicles registered from 1.4.69, the edges of the internal mirror must be covered by a protective material.

On all vehicles registered after 1.6.78 both the offside mirror and internal mirror must be capable of adjustment from the driving seat.

Close proximity wide angle rear-view mirrors may be fitted to the nearside of goods vehicles exceeding 12,000kg gross weight and this is obligatory for such vehicles first used from 1.10.88.

Similar to the instructions given under the heading of *Glass*, drivers should ensure that their mirrors are always clean and correctly positioned to give immediate viewing from the driving position.

NOISE

No motor vehicle or trailer which causes excessive noise may be used on the road, nor may it be used in a manner to cause excessive noise which could be avoided.

Noise or excessive noise emitted by a vehicle includes noise attributable to any load, burden, or goods carried and to the manner in which the load is fitted, as well as that emitted by an inefficient exhaust silencer device.

For the purpose of testing and inspection of vehicles on noise limits, levels are laid down in the construction and use regulations.

OPENING OF DOORS

It is an offence to open doors in such a manner as to cause injury or danger to other vehicles or persons.

SEAT BELTS

Goods vehicles not exceeding 1525kg unladen registered on or after 1.4.67, must be fitted with seat belts for the driver and one front passenger. These requirements also apply to cars first registered on or after 1.1.65, and three-wheeled vehicles weighing over 255kg registered on or after 1.9.70.

In addition, vehicles to which the regulations apply first used from 1.4.87 must, if they have any other forward facing front seats beside the driver's seat (ie bench seats) be fitted with seat belts. Cars and dual-purpose vehicles first used from this date must also have seat belts fitted to forward facing seats behind the driver's seat. All seat belts must bear the appropriate approval mark.

Seat belts and anchorage points must be maintained in a proper condition at all times and the area within 30cm of the anchorage points must be free of serious corrosion. distortion or fracture.

Seat belts must be worn by drivers and front seat passengers where compulsory fitting of seat belts applies.

Certain exemptions from these requirements are allowed especially for persons engaged in delivering and collecting goods or mail, ie local delivery rounds where short stopping journeys are involved; and also for the police when escorting civilians; for prison officers when escorting prisoners; and for firemen but only while putting on operational clothing or equipment whilst travelling to an emergency. A person may also be exempted on medical grounds provided they hold a valid certificate signed by a medical practitioner.

Responsibility for wearing a seat belt rests with each occupant of the vehicle but when children under the age of 14 are carried in the front seat it is the driver's responsibility.

Failure to comply with the regulations is an offence and carries a substantial fine on summary conviction.

SMOKE

Every motor vehicle must be so constructed that no avoidable smoke or visible vapour is emitted. Excess fuel devices must not be used on diesel engine vehicles whilst in action.

It is an offence to drive a vehicle which is emitting smoke or dangerous vapour.

SPEEDOMETERS

These must be fitted to all motor vehicles registered from 1.10.37 (vehicles with a speed up to 25 mph are exempt).

Speedometers must be maintained in good working order at all material times. If a defect develops steps should be taken to have it rectified as soon as possible.

There is no need to fit a separate speedometer when a vehicle is required to be fitted with a tachograph.

TACHOGRAPHS

In accordance with EC regulations tachographs should be fitted to all vehicles used for carrying goods exceeding 3.5 tonnes gross and vehicles adapted or constructed to carry more than 17 persons, (nine persons if the vehicle is used on international journeys) including the driver. (For more detailed information on tachographs see page 53.)

TOW-ROPES

If a tow-rope or chain is used to tow a vehicle it must not exceed 4.5m in length and it must be made visible from either side if it exceeds 1.5m in length.

TRAILERS

The varying types and designs of trailers used in connection with commercial vehicle operations fall into the following categories.

Drawbar trailers — of one and two axles with drawbar and bolt connection to the towing vehicle and also brake and lighting connections. With this type of trailer the connections have to be carried out manually.

Also included under this heading are heavy duty low-loader type trailers with single and twin rear axles and "knock-out" axles to facilitate the loading of heavy machinery, etc.

Semi-trailers — articulated trailers of one, two and three rear axles with automatic coupling and fifth wheel coupling gear for connecting to the towing vehicle.

The brakes and lighting connections on semi-trailers are made at the same time as the coupling gear is connected to the towing vehicle. Therefore, other than winding up the landing legs and releasing the trailer parking brake, the manual operations, compared with the drawbar trailer, are minimal.

The semi-trailer is predominantly used because of its flexibility and economy in operation, which has produced a very high utilisation in ratios of three trailers to one unit.

Despite these advantages there are, of course, some disadvantages and these invariably arise during the operation through neglect or carelessness in the driving or handling of the vehicle and trailer, or through lack of experience, or instability or insecurity of the load and, finally, through the lack of efficient maintenance.

The main legal requirements, such as brakes and lights, etc, have been covered in their respective sections, but the following additional safety factors should be observed.

1. The centre of gravity of the trailer and its load is higher than that of the motor vehicle and is, therefore, more likely to overturn if driven round bends and turns at excessive speed.

2. If speed and braking are not carefully observed when driving on unsatisfactory road surface conditions the semi-trailer is more subject to skidding than the rigid vehicle, and also to jack-knifing.

3. Uncoupling the trailer:
   (a) secure trailer brake in the "ON" position
   (b) lower front trailer legs and lock in position
   (c) release braking and electrical connections
   (d) release coupling.

4. Recoupling the trailer:
   (a) reverse tractive unit **slowly** into coupling position
   (b) ensure unit is securely coupled by attempting to move forward with trailer parking brake applied
   (c) connect braking and electrical connection
   (d) secure front trailer legs in "UP" position
   (e) release trailer parking brake.

Safety First
When picking up alternative trailers ensure that the brakes are efficient. The first duty after recoupling and moving off on a journey is to test the brakes.

TYRES

Requirements

It is illegal to use a tyre:

    (a) which is not correctly inflated

    (b) which has a break in its fabric or a cut in excess of 25mm or 10% of the section width of the tyres, deep enough to reach the body cords

    (c) which has a lump, bulge or tear caused by separation, etc

    (d) which is the wrong size or type for the vehicle's use

    (e) which has any portion of ply or cord exposed

    (f) on which the base of any groove which showed in the original tread pattern is not clearly visible

    (g) on which either (i) the grooves of the tread pattern do not have a depth of a least 1mm throughout a continuous band measuring at least ¾ of the breadth of tread and round the entire outer circumference of the tyre, or, (ii) where the original tread pattern did not extend beyond ¾ of the breadth of the tread, the base of any groove which showed in the tyre's original tread pattern does not have a depth of at least 1mm.

Note: It is also illegal to fit to motor vehicles having only two axles and equipped with one or two single wheels, tyres of different types, ie cross-ply, radial or bias-belted, in the following manners: (a) diagonal-ply tyres or bias-belted tyres on the rear axle and radial-ply tyres on the front axle, and (b) diagonal-ply tyres on the rear axle and bias-belted tyres on the front axle. This does not apply if wide tyres, other than those used for engineering plant, are fitted.

    Also, tyres of different structures must not be fitted to vehicles with (a) more than one steerable axle, or (b) more than one driven axle not being a steerable axle.

Maintenance of tyres

Although maintenance of tyres, like total vehicle maintenance is the responsibility of the maintenance staff, there are certain periodical checks that are the responsibility of the driver.

The following check list is therefore recommended.

Daily check

(a) Check tyre pressures (cold). Tyres generate heat during running and more so during hot weather, which may cause pressures to rise some 10 to 15 pounds above the recommended pressure

(b) examine tyres for cuts, blisters and stones, etc, especially between twin-tyres. At first sight any of these may not appear to be dangerous, but can extend to dangerous proportions in the course of a journey

(c) check twin rear tyres. Inner and outer tyres should have the same diameters and the same pressures. One twin tyre below pressure will cause overloading of the other and an eventual blow-out

(d) make sure that all tyres show a reasonable amount of tread pattern and that the spare wheel and tyre are in similar good order and inflated to the correct pressure.

Further information on this subject is given on page 172.

Note: it is illegal for tyre suppliers to sell car tyres unless the tyre has an "E" marking which shows compliance with load and speed requirements of ECE regulation 30. Also, *retreaded* car and lorry tyres are now illegal unless manufactured and marked in accordance with BS AU 144b: 1977. Drivers should ask a supplier to point out the marking on the tyre if they have to obtain a replacement whilst out on the road.

Tyre loads and speed ratings

Goods vehicles and trailers must be fitted with tyres designed to adequately support the maximum axle weight of each axle of the vehicle when driven at maximum speeds allowed for the particular class of vehicle (see page 79 for speed limits) except that in the case of a low platform trailer, a local authority road cleansing, watering or refuse collection vehicle, etc or a multi-stop local collection and delivery vehicle used only within a radius of 25 miles of its permanent base, the tyres must be adequate for speeds up to 40mph.

Tyre service and supply

For the benefit of operators or owner-drivers, the tyre manufacturers and their distributors offer substantial repair and replacement facilities. This information is available in booklet form issued free by the distributors and supervised by the National Tyre Distributors Association, Broadway House, The Broadway, London SW19.

The booklet of this association lists over 1100 depots of which around 700 offer a 24 hour service seven days a week.

A copy of the booklet should be included with other documents which are always carried on the vehicle.

Additional information concerning service and supply of tyres on the Continent of Europe can be found on page 219.

VEHICLE DIMENSIONS

The Road Vehicles (Construction and Use) Regulations deal with the construction, weight and equipment of vehicles.

For the benefit of those drivers who are new to commercial vehicle operation and persons commencing their studies in road transport activities, it is first necessary to define the meaning of certain expressions.

Definitions

Motor vehicle   A mechanically propelled vehicle intended or adapted for use on the roads.

Trailer   A vehicle drawn by a motor vehicle.

Goods Vehicle   A vehicle constructed or adapted for the carriage of goods, including trailers. Vehicles up to 3050kg unladen weight (3500kg with built-in gas propulsion equipment) are termed "motor cars".

Heavy motor car	A mechanically propelled vehicle, not being a motor car, constructed to carry a load or passengers having an unladen weight exceeding 2540kg.
Articulated vehicle	A motor car or heavy motor car with a trailer so attached that 20% of its load, when uniformly distributed, is borne by the drawing vehicle. For registration purposes it is regarded as one vehicle and excise duty payable is calculated on the plated weight and on the number of axles on the tractive unit and number of axles on the semi-trailer.
Motor tractor	A motor vehicle not constructed to carry a load, with an unladen weight not exceeding 7370kg.
Light locomotive	As above, but with an unladen weight over 7370kg up to 11,690kg.
Heavy locomotive	As above, but with an unladen weight over 11,690kg.
Dual-purpose vehicle	A vehicle constructed or adapted for the carriage either of passengers or goods or burden of any description with an unladen weight not exceeding 2040kg and which either is four-wheeled driven or meets specified requirements as to body construction.
Composite trailer	A combination of a converter dolly and a semi-trailer.
Converter dolly	A trailer with two or more wheels which allows a semi-trailer to move without any of its weight being superimposed on the drawing vehicle and which itself is not part of either the semi-trailer or the drawing vehicle.
OAS	Outer axle spread.

IAS	Inner axle spread.
GVW	Gross vehicle weight.
GCW	Gross combination weight.
GTW	Gross train weight.

These definitions will be of value when dealing with vehicle selection when the choice of *axle spread, axle loading and gross vehicle weight* has to be made.

Maximum vehicle dimensions
Length

Rigid vehicle	12m
Articulated vehicle	15.5m (16.5m depending on distance between king pin and rear of semi-trailer)
	18m where the semi-trailer is a low-loader (other than a step frame low-loader)
Trailer	7m but this is increased to 12m for a trailer which:
	(a) has not less than four wheels and the distance between the points of contact with the road of the fore-most and rearmost wheels on the same side is not less than three-fifths of its overall length and
	(b) is drawn by a motor vehicle having an unladen weight of 2030kg or more.
Road train (vehicle and one trailer)	18m* (Where a broken-down vehicle is being towed by a motor vehicle the overall combination may exceed 18m.)
Road train (vehicle and two trailers)	25.9m

*18.35m for close-coupled drawbar trailer combinations from 1.10.91.

Width

Goods vehicle and dual-purpose vehicle	2.5m
Refrigerated vehicle	specially designed for carrying goods at low temperatures and having side walls, including insulation, at least 45mm thick — 2.6m.
Trailer (with exceptions)	2.3m
Trailer (drawn by a motor vehicle having a plated maximum weight exceeding 3500kg)	2.5m
Motor tractor	2.5m
Locomotive	2.75m

Height

Not specified for goods vehicles, except the following — if the semi-trailer has a plated gross weight exceeding 26,000kg and the *total laden weight* of the semi-trailer plus the tractive unit when driven on the road exceeds 32,520kg, a height limit of 4.2m applies.

This height limit includes the structure of the vehicle and any detachable structure attached to the vehicle for containing the load, for instance a container. It does not include any load which is not a detachable structure or any sheeting or other flexible means of covering or securing the load.

Maximum overhang

Goods vehicles   60% of wheelbase.

Motor tractors   1.83m.

Note: only locomotives and motor tractors may tow more than one trailer.

RESPONSIBILITIES OF A GOOD DRIVER

A driver's responsibilities in connection with the driving of his vehicle and the delivery of its load, are very involved and carry heavy obligations. Both the general public and the employer look to the driver to do a "professional job".

From the commencement of driving duties, or from carrying out the vehicle "checks" before moving off, he is concerned with **safety**.

Safety — for the vehicle and its load.
Safety — for delivery of the goods to customer's premises and correct documentation.
Safety — to other road users in the course of driving duties.

Many of the goods vehicle driver's responsibilities are covered under the respective sections throughout this book, but there are others of equal importance which are outlined below

1. Driving offences and endorsements whilst on duty must be reported.

2. Driving licences (especially those containing LGV entitlement, or HGV licences) must be renewed at the appropriate time and be available for the manager's inspection if required.

3. Unauthorised persons are not to be carried on vehicles.

4. Up to three blameworthy accidents can result in dismissal, each case being dealt with on merit.

5. All vehicle accidents must be reported promptly with complete details as requested on the insurance company's accident form.

6. Fuel pumps and governor seals must not be interfered with.

7. Statutory breaks will be taken on the road or at base, as instructed.

8. The conditions applicable to meat contracts in respect of payments, security, and hygiene must be complied with when employed on such work.

9. Checking loads on and off a vehicle is the responsibility of the driver. At certain delivery points (eg cold stores) where goods are taken away to stows a re-check is not always practicable if there is a disagreement between the checker and the driver. The driver should therefore agree, item by item, with the checker, to eliminate any doubt.

10. Signing for loads is most important and drivers must be careful to sign only for the quantities actually received, and endorse the signature note in respect of any discrepancies or damage.

11. Drivers' daily hours of work records (in most cases this is the tachograph chart) must be completed correctly.

12. Seals attached to the tachograph must not be tampered with.

13. Refuelling of vehicles must be completed at the termination of the day's work, or before commencement of the following day's work.
    Fuel will not be drawn on the road except in an emergency, when a receipt will be submitted, or an agency card used.

14. Parking: vehicles are to be parked in an authorised vehicle park and tickets obtained. Vehicles must not be parked in the streets.

15. Courtesy at all times is essential, both on the road and on customers' premises. Drivers should remember that they are representatives of their company and should conduct themselves accordingly.

16. The operator's licence must always be displayed in a conspicuous place on the vehicle. Drivers and staff should remember that vehicles should not be loaded if a licence disc is not displayed.

17. Communication by telephone is essential to operational efficiency and no time should be lost in contacting the transport office in the event of delays, and on arrival at the destination for instructions for return loads.

Instructions in respect of set times to telephone depots may be issued by managers to suit local requirements.

18. Perishable goods are to be delivered with the utmost care and expediency. Delays, or the possibility of maximum hours being worked before delivery can be completed, must be reported immediately to the transport manager.

19. Drivers are expected to work on general duties in the yard, or on the loading bank when not employed on driving duties.

20. Uniforms or overalls, when issued, should be worn at all times when on duty.

21. Meetings in respect of trade union matters are not to be held on company premises without the permission of the manager.

22. Dangerous loads. Drivers of tanker vehicles must see that the vehicle is showing the correct warning panels or compartment labels when carrying dangerous substances and that the Tremcard(s) are available in the cab.

Drivers of vehicles carrying dangerous substances in packages must see that the reflectorised orange plates are fitted to the vehicle and that the Tremcard(s) covering the substances are available in the cab.

Fire extinguishers. Vehicles carrying dangerous substances must be equipped with an extinguisher which, in the first instance, is capable of dealing with a fire in the engine. Extinguishers able to deal with a fire in the load are also advisable. The driver, however, should not attempt to deal with a chemical, etc., fire unless he has had formal training in the correct method of using fire fighting equipment. (See pages 191–8 for more detailed information on the carriage of dangerous substances.)

23. Security of loads. Drivers are responsible for safety of

loads, particularly high loads and timber haulage, sheeting of loads, and locking and sealing box bodies when carrying valuable cargo.

Regulation 100 of the Construction and Use regulations is a wide ranging regulation which requires the driver (and the operator) to ensure that **all** loads are made secure, ie loose loads must be sheeted and all loads physically restrained, other than by their own weight, if necessary, to ensure that they do not cause a **danger** or **nuisance** to persons or property by either shifting or being blown from the vehicle or trailer. If a load does shift or fall from the vehicle the driver will be liable to prosecution for having an "insecure load" and his employer can also face heavy fines.

Similarly, if the vehicle is found to be overloaded (which is an absolute offence) both the driver and the employer will be liable to prosecution.

In such incidents not only does the driver jeopardise his HGV licence, or LGV entitlement but the employer can be called before the Traffic Commissioner who issued the operator's licence to explain such occurrences.

24. Particular care must be taken when sheeting and handling vehicles with fragile loads.

25. **Where anti-theft devices are fitted to vehicles, these must be operated in positive control whenever a vehicle is left loaded and unattended. This is very necessary to safeguard insurance claims**.

Maintenance checks

It is the prime duty of all persons intending to drive motor vehicles to acquaint themselves with the fundamental working principles of maintenance requirements. Not all drivers will be sufficiently mechanically minded to appreciate their maintenance responsibilities, but it is most necessary — in the interest of public safety — that they be trained in, or acquire a basic knowledge of, these requirements.

The law demands that a driver of a motor vehicle must not drive a vehicle that is in an unsound mechanical condition.

Responsibilities covering maintenance checks fall into two categories.

1. Checking of equipment before commencement of a day's work or a distant journey:

   (a) fuel, oil and water
   (b) fan belt
   (c) brakes
   (d) tyre condition and inflation pressures, spare wheel and jack
   (e) driving mirrors, windscreen-wipers and washers
   (f) lights and reflectors
   (g) stop lights and indicators
   (h) steering.

2. Items connected with daily or weekly checks and vehicle operation, but requiring more detailed instruction:
   (a) tyre and wheel changing
   (b) care and attention of batteries
   (c) all controls within the cab (lighting controls and connection)
   (d) water-cooling system and the use of antifreeze
   (e) fuel supply, checking and clearing air locks (diesel fuel system)
   (f) cold-starting procedure
   (g) brake and light coupling systems (for trailers and articulated vehicles)
   (h) special equipment and controls used with tankers, tail-lifts, autocranes, etc
   (i) appreciation of refrigeration systems and controls.
   (j) fire extinguishers (in relation to dangerous goods in tanks or in packaged form).

Whatever arrangements are made by the operator for the efficient maintenance and servicing of his vehicles, ultimately it is the driver who is responsible for reporting on performance. He, more than anyone else, handles the vehicle under load, which is one time when a true test of the vehicle's performance may be obtained.

With the heavy increases in fines for offences relating to vehicles it cannot be over-emphasised how important it is for

112

the driver to ensure as much as possible that the vehicle is roadworthy, is not overloaded and that the goods being carried are secure. Equally, he must observe the drivers' hours rules and complete his tachograph charts correctly (for this last item refer to pages 53–62.

AUTOMATIC TRANSMISSION

Automatic or semi-automatic methods of transmission are not, as many people think, fairly recent innovations. In various forms they have been used in cars, buses and coaches for a number of years, although the principal development has been in the United States.

Fully-automatic transmission has developed to a fair degree of efficiency and is a popular fitment in cars and light vans. With the easier driving controls taking much of the fatigue out of driving, and particularly the "stop start" work in heavy traffic conditions, this form of transmission is very popular with drivers.

The various systems are outlined so that readers may obtain some appreciation of the working principles.

Borg-Warner automatic transmission

For most makes of cars and light vans the fitting of automatic transmission is optional eg the Borg-Warner is a fluid drive type which operates ideally on all gears, being the only automatic transmission for medium size cars and vans which includes a "park" position on the selector plus a "push-start" and "tow". It also has advantages for trailer-towing equipment. Cars and vans fitted with this type of transmission have two pedals only and a selector which provides the following driving range:

Park

Reverse

Neutral

Normal or Drive

Lock up.

Normal driving control of the vehicle is carried out by means of two pedals. Some 60% of the driving worries are eliminated, difficulties of gear-changing are forgotten, and maximum attention can be paid to road procedure.

Starting on a hill becomes an easy and pleasant task and it is practically impossible to stall the engine. Automatic transmissions can, of course, be more expensive than the conventional gearbox, and fuel consumption is higher. However, because engine revolutions are controlled, wear and tear on the engine is reduced and there are no clutch repairs.

The drive position is used for normal motoring and the gear automatically changes from first to second and second to third depending on the acceleration. The gears change in reverse order with the reduction of engine speed.

Driving away from rest — (1) Start engine; (2) move lever to D; (3) accelerate; (4) release handbrake. (As the car increases speed all other changes will be made to suit the car's speed and torque demand.)

L (Lock-up position) — In this position first gear is "locked" with maximum engine braking until the driver selects the drive position when the gear will automatically change in accordance with road speed. If the driver wishes to "lock" second gear, this can be done immediately returning the lever from D to L. If travelling at speeds *over* 20 mph and an immediate change-down to second gear is required, then L should be selected and the immediate change will be effected. If travelling at *up to* 20 mph the same procedure can be carried out and the transmission will "lock" in first gear.

N (Neutral position) — In this position the vehicle may be towed, coasted, or started.

P (Park) — The transmission is in "neutral" and the car is mechanically "locked" against movement. Always move the lever to this position when the car is parked or if the engine is left running for any length of time when adjustments and tuning are to be carried out.

D and R (Drive and Reverse) — Used quickly and alternately, the resulting rocking motion will extract the car from soft ground.

Kick-down — When intending to climb a hill or overtake another vehicle and a quick burst of acceleration and extra power is required, depress the accelerator pedal as far as possible beyond the full throttle position. Transmission will then change down from top to intermediate and will remain there until the accelerator is released. If a long climb is anticipated, or extensive use of a low ratio is required, the manual "low" should be used and engaged when the road speed is below 30 mph.

Stopping — The vehicle should be stopped in the normal way by applying the foot brake, leaving the control lever at D until stationary. Move the lever to N or P and apply the handbrake.

The Allison Automatics
These automatics provide many advantages for drivers of vehicles which must "stop and go" much of the time or encounter driving conditions requiring frequent speed changes.

Allison Transmission offer full automatic models for truck and buses operating on gasoline, diesel or gas turbine engines ranging up to 400 horsepower. GVW ratings range up to 80,000 pounds and GCW ratings up to 130,000 pounds.

There are two principle component groups in the Allison Automatic transmission — the torque converter and the planetary gearing system. A third major component, the hydraulic control valve body, is the "brain" of the transmission.

The pump, turbine and stator comprise the torque converter section. The convertor multiplies engine torque at low speeds and under heavy loads. Oil flow is the key factor in the mechanism.

The transmission "range selector positions" are:

    R— reverse
    N— neutral position

D— drive (in all gears)
3— occasionally the road, load or traffic conditions will make it desirable to restrict the automatic
2— shifting to a lower range
1— low gear (use when pulling through mud and snow or driving up steep gradients).

In the lower ranges (1, 2 and 3), the transmission will not upshift above the highest gear selected unless the recommended engine governed speed for that gear is exceeded.

Driving tips
Pressure of the foot on the accelerator pedal influences the automatic shifting. When the pedal is fully depressed against the pedal stop on the floor, the transmission will automatically upshift near the recommended governed speed of the engine. A partially depressed position of the pedal will cause the upshifts to occur sooner at a lesser engine speed.

Downshift control
The transmission can be downshifted or upshifted, even at full throttle and although there is no speed limitation on upshifting there is a limit on downshifting and reverse. Good driving practices indicate that downshifting should be avoided when the vehicle is above the maximum speed attainable in the next lower gear.

The built-in downshift inhibitors within the valve body prevent those harmful shifts when the vehicle is going too fast for the next lower gear. If down shifts are attempted at excessive speeds, the inhibitors prevent the selected downshift until the vehicle reaches an acceptable speed.

Using the engine to slow the vehicle
To use the engine as a braking force, shift the range selector to the next lower stage. If the vehicle is exceeding the maximum speed for a lower gear, use the service brakes to slow the vehicle to an acceptable speed where the transmission may be *down-shifted* safely.

Towing or pushing

Before towing or pushing a disabled vehicle, the *drive* should be disconnected or the drive wheels lifted off the road. The engine cannot be started by pushing or towing.

Parking brake

There is no "park" position in the transmission shift pattern, therefore always use the parking brake to hold the vehicle when unattended.

Oil temperatures must be observed and some vehicles are installed with a gauge specifically designed for this purpose.

Normal operating temperatures are between 160°-220°F.

The SCG automatic control

This fully automatic gear selection system for passenger vehicles and trucks is designed by Self-Changing Gears Ltd of Coventry.

The equipment provides, for pneumocyclic gear boxes, an automatic gear selection system with smooth and uninterrupted shift action. This is achieved by the association of air pressure modulating valves with an electric circuit, used in conjunction with electro-pneumatic gear selection valves with large airways. This circuit is housed in a control panel connected by cables to a driver's direction selector switch, an accelerator pedal controlled switch, a magnet valve unit comprising the gear selection, pressure modulating and relaxing valves, and a speed generator.

The circuit energies the gear selection valves in sequence as the vehicle speed rises so that gear ratios appropriate to the speed are always used, and both "racing" and "labouring" of the engine are avoided.

When an "up" gear shift occurs, air is released rapidly from the cylinder of the gear already in use and is with equal rapidity admitted at high pressure to the cylinder of the succeeding gear so that the associated brake band is brought into action on to near dry drum with maximum effect in minimum time.

Simultaneously with the operation of the gear selector valve the modulating valve exhausts and in so doing causes a rapid

117

reduction in the air pressure. This coincides with the rapid increase in the coefficient of friction and compensates for it, producing an extremely consistent level of torque, falling smoothly from one gear to the next.

When the shift has been completed the modulating valves restore the high pressure level in anticipation of the next shift.

If required a selector with a shift for operating doors on buses automatically can be optioned.

The ZF Transmatic-Transmission

This unique auto-transmission comprises four major components: an hydraulic torque converter, a lock-up converter clutch, a shift clutch and a five or six speed ZF synchromesh gearbox. So in theory the driver has the best of both worlds — hence the name "Transmatic".

Moving off
The technique for starting off fully laden is to select second (or possibly third) gear in the usual way after depressing the clutch pedal. Releasing the clutch does not cause the vehicle to move, as slip between the engine idle speed and the stationary vehicle is absorbed by the convertor.

Depressing the accelerator allows the vehicle to move away smoothly. As soon as a certain vehicle speed and its corresponding engine speed have been reached, the lock-up clutch is actuated automatically, providing a direct connection between engine and gearbox.

Motoring
If required, the Transmatic can be driven like a normal synchromesh gearbox, ie depress the clutch, select the gear, release the clutch.

Kick-down
When the engine has nothing more to give (at less than 1500 rpm for instance) there is no need to change down to the next lower gear. All that is required is to advance the accelerator down to the boards to select "kick-down", which immediately

opens the converter and produces increased vehicle traction. This is indicated by the yellow pilot lamp coming on. Should the increased traction provided by converter operation no longer be required, the converter is automatically "locked-up" again thus causing the pilot lamp to extinguish.

Stopping and moving off again

The Transmatic convertor allows the driver to stop the vehicle in any gear without having to use the clutch — just the footbrake. The correct gear will automatically be selected for the vehicle to move off again by releasing the footbrake and accelerating.

Appreciation

The simplicity of stepless power transmission gives drivers decisive advantages. Gear changing is reduced by as much as 9% with considerable reduction in driver fatigue.

Even when the going gets really tough, there is always a smooth, no fuss getaway with the Transmatic, which not only takes the heat out of the clutch, but is capable of increasing engine torque more than twofold.

As with automatic transmission systems generally, users and fleet owners profit from the Transmatic by a reduction in fuel consumption, clutch repairs, vehicle down time plus extended engine life.

The Eaton Twin Splitter Transmission

The Twin Splitter Transmission manufactured by Eaton Ltd., of Manchester, consists of a main box with four forward gears and one reverse gear and an auxiliary box with three splitter gears. Each gear can be split three times for a total of twelve evenly spaced forward and three reverse gears. Operation is by a single H pattern gear lever. Each splitter gear can be preselected and brought into action at precise synchronous speed by operating the throttle without necessarily using the clutch.

Only four lever movements are required to reach cruising speed. All further gear changes are preselected with the splitter switch. The substantial reduction in physical effort improves the driver's performance and makes driving more economical and safer by allowing him more time to concentrate on the road ahead.

The Twin Splitter Transmission is fitted with an upshift brake for faster upshifts, of particular benefit with a fully laden vehicle on an incline.

Driving

The splitter positions are:

    I — Low
    II — Intermediate
    III — High

Upshifts
To start: preselect splitter I,
      depress clutch pedal to fullest extent,
      shift to first lever position,
      release clutch/apply throttle.

To make a splitter upshift only:

      preselect splitter II or III,
      depress/release clutch,
      alternatively release throttle momentarily,
      apply throttle.

To make a compound (lever and splitter together) upshift:

      preselect splitter I,
      shift lever to next position while double declutching,
      apply throttle.

Downshift:

      preselect splitter II or I
      depress/release clutch (do not depress to fullest extent)
      alternatively release throttle momentarily,
      re-apply throttle immediately.

To make a compound upshift:

> preselect splitter III,
> shift lever to next lever position
> while double declutching,
> (do not depress to fullest extent)
> apply throttle.

For full driving instructions, the driver should consult the Driver Instructions Booklet.

The Eaton SAMT Transmission

The SAMT Transmission is a semi-automatic derivative of the Twin Splitter Transmission that retains driver control while reducing effort and stress to a minimum. The core concept is improved driveline management; monitoring the road speed, transmission ratio and throttle position and elaying that information to the driver in an easily understood form via a visual gear display.

The gear display shows the gear engaged and by means of arrows, the number of gears available for shifting up or down.

The conventional gear lever is replaced by a gear selector which can be finger tip operated for all up and down changes as well as skip shifts.

Driving

The starting gear (up to five gears available) is selected by depressing the clutch pedal and flicking the gear selector up to the required gear. The clutch is not used for any subsequent gear change.

During gear changes the throttle position can be maintained since the engine speed requires no adjustment by the throttle. Gears are changed by simply moving the gear selector once for an upshift or downshift.

The selected gear engages automatically. The SAMT Transmission only accept shifts indicated on the display by upwards or downwards pointing arrows.

If the display indicates more than one gear available either up or down, gears can be skipped easily by simply moving the lever twice or three times in quick succession.

When slowing down there is no need to go through all the gears individually. Simply stay in gear until the engine revs fall to approximately 1000rpm and then move the lever down once. The system automatically selects the appropriate gear for the vehicle road speed.

When coming to rest from a high gear, one lever movement down, with the clutch depressed, will automatically select neutral or one of the low gears, depending on vehicle specification.

The SAMT Transmission does not accept a signal that could take the engine out of its programmed working range.

For detailed driving instructions for the SAMT Transmission, refer to the Driver Instructions booklet.

Diagnostics
The SAMT Transmission incorporates a diagnostic system which permanently supervises the driveline operating conditions.

Any malfunction is reported instantly through the gear display, allowing fast, precise corrective action to be taken.

THE TWO-SPEED AXLE

This is an extremely useful piece of machinery which usually is either completely mishandled or rarely fully exploited. Many drivers are never taught to use the two-speed axle according to manufacturers' instructions and this omission has a more detrimental effect when more than one driver operates a particular vehicle, because varying standards of handling can ruin this equipment.

Two-speed axles are operated by air-pressure, vacuum or electric mechanisms with a shift button attached to the gear lever. This control effects a change from high to low ratio (or vice versa) and gives double the number of gears compared with the standard gearbox. In the case of a five-speed transmission this gives 10 forward and two reverse gears. By selecting the correct combination to suit road conditions and the weight of load carried, the engine will "pull" more efficiently and economically. Over the majority of trunk-road routes, average speeds should be considerably higher and the driver will experience much less fatigue.

The correct use of the two-speed axle will certainly reduce to a minimum any repair work brought about by unnecessary wear and tear in driving.

The two-speed axle is quite a common fitting on commercial vehicles — some manufacturers supply it as standard equipment, others as an optional extra.

Many drivers think that the high-ratio top is to be used purely as an overdrive and that little benefit is to be gained by using the high and low shifts in the intermediate gears. This is a very misguided opinion, by not using the equipment to full advantage the vehicle's maximum road performance and fuel economy are rarely achieved. It is therefore proposed to detail the operating instructions.

Shifting from high to low ratio

Before a transport driver can use the two-speed rear axle efficiently, he must understand the reasons for making a shift from one ratio to another and the correct method of operation in order to get the best from his vehicle.

To shift into low speed ratio:

(a) keep accelerator down, push button down

(b) to complete shift, disengage and re-engage clutch as *quickly* as possible, keeping accelerator pedal down. (See Fig. 1).

The following will explain in greater detail the advantage of a clutch-operated shift to low ratio. Let us assume that a fully-laden vehicle is approaching a steep hill where a gear change is obviously imminent. (It is most important here to maintain engine revolutions.) The driver is in high top gear. As soon as the engine shows signs of "labouring", he should drop into low

123

top (using the clutch method) and if a further change is called for, he should bring into operation the split-change. Change down progressively, ie 5-high/5-low, maybe 4-high/4-low, and so on.

This will enable the vehicle to maintain a fair speed and provide power to "clear" the hill. By the time a gear as low as third is required speed will not be so important as power, and the use of the low-ratio gears will provide this power.

Use of the low-ratio gears in conjunction with the normal high-ratio set will enable maximum torque to be maintained throughout the period of driving under difficult conditions.

Naturally a good deal of practice is required before a driver is able to judge a gradient, make rapid high to low ratio shifts and take best advantage of the two-speed rear axle. Nevertheless the effort required is well worthwhile and advantages to both driver and operator are considerble.

Shifting from low to high ratio

1. Keep accelerator pedal down, pull button up.
2. To complete shift, *release accelerator and disengage clutch at the same time* (See Fig. 2)

Split shifting

1. To shift into the next higher gear in the gearbox and at the same time from high to low ratio — make the gearbox shift in the usual way and just before engaging the clutch move the button *down*.
2. To shift into the next lower gear in the gearbox and at the same time from low to high axle ratio — with the accelerator down move the button up, then complete the gearbox shift in the usual way (see Fig. 3).

A further example of split-shifting is as follows. A driver is in fourth low and needs more power and also more speed. He should change to the next lower gear in transmission (third) and *at the same time* change from low to high speed ratio (see Fig. 4).

Important

1. Always keep accelerator pedal down when axle control button is moved except when split-shifting to low-axle ratio.

2. Always start truck in low-axle ratio.

3. Always park truck in low-axle ratio.

Conclusion

Remember that, efficiently operated, a two-speed axle can considerably lengthen the life of a heavy commercial vehicle and the driver will be able to maintain a higher standard of driving with much less physical effort. However, the secret of success lies in intelligent anticipation of road conditions.

With increasingly heavy traffic conditions and the strain on drivers increasing proportionately, the driver of a heavy commercial vehicle fitted with the two-speed rear axle should make a point of completely familiarising himself with this valuable equipment for the benefit of his vehicle, his employer and himself.

Fig.1

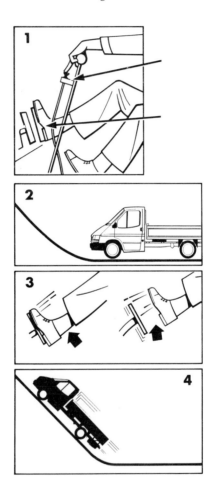

Fig. 1

TWO-SPEED AXLE

Changing from **high** to **low** ratio

Diagram 1: Just before you need to change — push the button *down* (or *in*) keeping accelerator pedal *down*.

Diagrams 2 and 3: Ride with accelerator *down* — disengage and re-engage clutch as quickly as possible.

Diagram 4: You have now changed to *low* speed axle ratio.

Fig.2

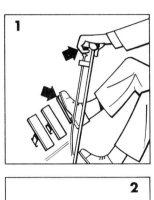

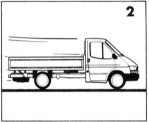

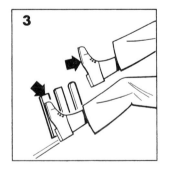

Fig.2

TWO-SPEED AXLE

Changing from **low** to **high** ratio

Diagram 1: Just before you wish to change, keeping accelerator pedal *down*, pull button *up* (or *out*).

Diagram 2: Ride with accelerator *down*.

Diagram 3: Release accelerator pedal. Disengage clutch at the same time and then re-engage clutch immediately. You have now changed to *high* speed axle ratio.

Fig.3

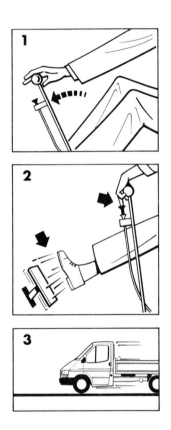

Fig. 3

TWO-SPEED AXLE

Split-gear changing

You are driving in third gear ratio but need more speed. If a change is made into fourth gear power is lost — so you need to change to the next higher gear in the transmission and, at the same time, from high to low speed axle ratio.

Diagram 1: Make gear change in usual way, then:

Diagram 2: Before engaging clutch, push button *down* and complete gear change.

Diagram 3: You have now changed to the next higher gear of the transmission and, at the same time, from high to low speed axle ratio.

Fig. 4

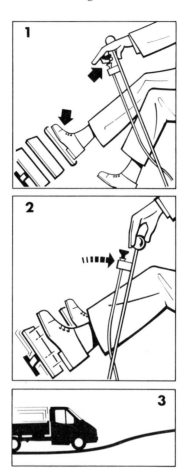

Fig. 4

TWO-SPEED AXLE

Spilt-gear changing (power and speed)

You are in fourth-low gear and need more power, but you also need more speed — so change to next lower gear in the transmission and at the same time, from low to high speed axle ratio.

Diagram 1: Pull the button up, keeping the accelerator pedal down.

Diagram 2: Complete gear change.

Diagram 3: You have now changed to the next lower gear in the transmission and, at the same time, from low to high speed axle ratio.

ARTICULATED VEHICLES

Trainees should be experienced in driving rigid motor vehicles before advancing to articulated vehicles. Therefore instruction in this chapter will relate only to the handling techniques for this equipment.

The operational advantages of articulated vehicles are manoeuvrability and flexibility which, with multiple-trailer operation, produce better vehicle and driver productivity.

In general, the handling procedure is much the same for all classes but variation will be experienced in manoeuvrability — particularly reversing. The reversing procedures illustrated are therefore based on heavy-duty vehicles, as these are considered more difficult to handle.

Classification of couplings
There are two principal types of coupling fitted to articulated vehicles:

(a) the automatic coupling

(b) the fifth wheel coupling.

Generally speaking, automatic couplings are used for payloads of up to 11 or 12 tons and the fifth wheel over these weights.

Fifth wheel coupling
This coupling is designed to meet safety requirements in carriage of heavier loads calling for a wider coupling plate, heavy-duty brakes, and independent trailer-support legs. With the exception of the actual coupling procedure, the remaining operations, (ie coupling and uncoupling of airbrake lines and

Automatic coupling
As the name implies this coupling provides speedy "make-and-break" between tractor and trailer with automatic contacts for brake and lighting systems. The complete operations of coupling and uncoupling can be controlled by the driver from within the cab, except for the need to apply and release the parking brake of the semi-trailer.

light cables) have to be handled by the driver from outside the cab and this also applies to the releasing of coupling lock when disconnecting.

Some trailer manufacturers market their own variations of the standard fifth wheel coupling gear with modified arrangements for air-brake lines and electric cable connections. One manufacturer in particular (Scammel) markets an automatic fifth wheel coupling gear with air operated trailer-support legs. These operations are controlled by the driver from the cab.

Mention is made of these different coupling arrangements to ensure that drivers fully appreciate the various applications in relation to the type of equipment they will be called upon to operate.

Driving responsibilities
Certain responsibilities peculiar to articulated vehicles must be observed. By design, the articulated vehicle, on comparative payload basis, will be longer than the rigid vehicle and turns and bends should therefore be taken at wider angles. Particular attention also must be paid to nearside view when turning left and overtaking.

Be especially careful when steering on three-quarter lock as, at this stage, the angle of the tractor obscures the view in the nearside mirror.

Caution should be exercised when driving downhill, on bends and wet road surfaces. Avoid sudden braking as, under these conditions, trailer "slide" can develop. Trailer "slide" is also possible where the brakes of tractor and trailer are not correctly balanced. This means that if the brakes of either the tractor rear wheels or the trailer wheels react forcibly, then wheel lock and skid will ensue. If the braking effort is not eased, the sliding motion of the trailer will increase and, in extreme cases, the trailer will slide at right angles to the tractor. This is known as "jack-knifing", the effects of which should not be considered a weakness inherent in articulated

(continued on page 138)

Fig.5

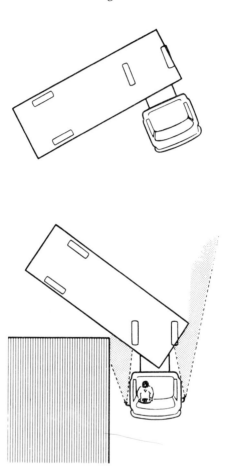

136

Fig. 5

JACK-KNIFING

This illustrates the position of tractor and trailer by the development of trailer "slide" and skidding. Also the resulting position of tractor by over-steering the reversing manoeuvres.

(continued from page 135)

vehicle braking systems. On the contrary, the systems are quite satisfactory but they must be maintained and balanced to the required standard. "Jack-knifing" and the conditions under which it occurs are exampled, so that drivers may fully appreciate what can happen if the vehicle is driven without due care and attention (see Fig. 5).

Hydraulic stabilisers are sometimes fitted to reduce the possibility of "jack-knifing" but in spite of the advantages offered by this equipment, it does incur additional handling time during coupling and uncoupling operations. It is considered that, except for vehicles with badly balanced brakes, the remedy to "jack-knifing" is in the hands of the driver and if the lessons laid down are thoroughly assimilated and practised then "jack-knifing" will be a very infrequent occurrence.

Keen observation of the road and traffic conditions and driving at speeds relative to those conditions are the controlling factors.

Brakes

The balancing of brakes between tractor and trailer is most important but can sometimes be problematical with multi-trailer operation. Although the manufacturer's design and systems are to the required standard, in operation the working efficiency can vary according to the standard of maintenance applied by vehicle operations.

For example, the brakes on a new trailer will react far differently from those on a trailer which has completed many miles of service. Both trailers could be towed by a tractor with efficient brakes and yet the braking reaction could differ in each case.

With multiple-trailer operation it is necessary that regular testing and adjustment be carried out.

As a precaution drivers should, before commencing a journey, carry out a short brake test after coupling-up to a fresh trailer.

Reversing

Reversing of articulated vehicles is more complex than with rigid vehicles but after reasonable practice experienced drivers become very adept in the movement.

Articulated vehicles can be reversed in a more confined area although by design the wheelbase and overall length of these vehicles is greater than that of their rigid counterparts.

The reversing instructions cover the total classification of trailers from 3 tonnes to 24 tonnes carrying capacity and the reversing manoeuvre therefore calls for precise handling as the range covers vehicles with overall lengths of from 20 to 42 feet (approximately 7m to 16m) with varying wheelbase measurements. Also in use are articulated vehicles with payloads in excess of those given, and these come under the authorisation of Special Types, including low-load and special transporter trailers for machinery etc.

According to size and payload, trailers will be fitted with one or more axles. On lightweight trailers a single axle with single wheels is usually the accepted standard. With medium and heavy trailers, twin wheels and additional axles are fitted to conform to loading requirements.

With multi-wheeled semi-trailers, the reaction to steering lock is somewhat slower in the reversing movements. This is caused by weight and size of trailers to be manoeuvred and to what is known as "drag" or "scuffing" of tyres. These points particularly are mentioned because, although the diagrams on reversing illustrate the principal methods of this movement, in practice the positioning of the steering lock and trailer could vary in certain cases.

Reversing applications

On the test, the requirements for reversing an articulated vehicle would not be the same as those for a rigid type vehicle. Although both applications require the driver to prove his efficiency in reversing vehicles into a side street or confined entry, in the case of articulated vehicles, additional requirements are called for.

In the course of his duties the driver will be called upon to carry out reversing manoeuvres in varied and exacting conditions under which it would not always be possible completely to execute the manoeuvres illustrated in the diagrams. Approaches to premises, stores, loading banks, warehouses and docks will vary greatly and will be a severe test of the driver's skill.

To reverse an articulated vehicle in one uninterrupted movement is therefore considered to be more of a refinement than a practical task. There is no reason why this should not be carried out but the manoeuvre can only be completed where there is ample space of uninterrupted movement. The method really can only be effectively employed with the use of light and medium class vehicles (see Fig. 6).

Double reverse manoeuvre
For practical purposes, the double reverse manoeuvre is recommended as illustrated in Figs. 7 and 8. Remember that it is the trailer itself which must be reversed and must closely be observed during the complete operation as the rear wheels of the tractor unit have to be "swung" in the opposite direction to the line to be taken by the rear of the trailer. "Over-steer" or excess "lock" should be avoided to prevent "jack-knifing" developing and the steering should be "swung" slightly the other way as soon as the trailer is seen to move on its intended course. A useful tip is to apply the steering lock in a "snaking" movement as indicated by the broken lines in the diagrams. The degree of modulation will be determined by observing the course of the trailer, the line of approach to the reverse point and, of course, the angle developed by tractor manoeuvrability.

Precautions to be observed with coupling gear
The responsibilities relating to the application of coupling gear are explained below.

1. When parking trailers, the coupling should not be broken at an angle as the re-coupling procedure is more difficult and accidents can result.

2. Ensure that the trailer parking brake is on before uncoupling and off after recoupling and before driving away.

3. With fifth wheel couplings ensure that the safety pin is secure before driving away.

4. Support legs must be lowered to full extent before uncoupling and fully raised and secured on recoupling and before driving away.

5. In the event of trailers having to be parked for any length of time on soft ground, suitable pieces of timber should be placed under the support legs. With loaded trailers the wheels, or feet, on the legs are liable to bend if not supported. Although penetration into the ground may be only slight it is, nevertheless, likely to affect clearance between trailer fifth wheel plate and tractor plate and this will obstruct recoupling. With the Scammell heavy-duty automatic coupling, special attention should be paid to the thickness of timber used; if this is too thick it will prevent the automatic coupling from locking in the *down* position.

6. Regularly check light and brake connections on automatic couplings.

7. Ensure that you fully understand the braking systems and the importance of correctly coupling-up the air-brake lines on two and three air-line systems. (As a visual aid, the connections usually are painted in distinctive colours, yellow for service, red for emergency, blue for third line.)

8. Tractors and trailers with different braking systems should not be connected or driven no matter how short the journey, as this will result in tractor brakes only being serviceable.

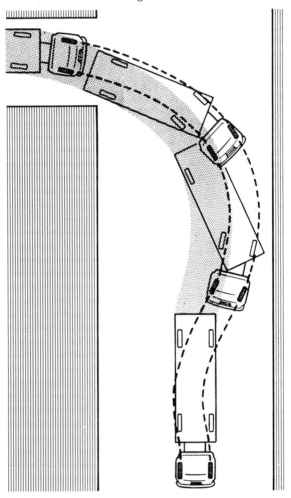

Fig. 6

142

Fig.6

SINGLE-MANOEUVRE REVERSING AN ARTICULATED VEHICLE

Reversing an articulated vehicle in one uninterrupted movement can only successfully be achieved on the right-hand reverse. The area over which the vehicle is to be reversed should be of sufficient width and clear of obstruction. The broad continuous line represents the line of travel for the complete manoeuvre. The broken line and angle of the steering wheels indicate the course of the steering manoeuvre.

Steering should be gently applied by "swinging" left and right alternately in a "snaking" movement. To keep the trailer on the "broad line" course (thus avoiding over-steering), observe closely the nearside rear wheels and the rear of the trailer throughout the manoeuvre, occasionally glancing in the nearside mirror and to the rear wheels of the tractor.

If "over-steer" develops it is better to stop, drive forward, and reposition the vehicle rather than to continue on the wrong course and finish in a "jack-knife" position.

Fig. 7(a)

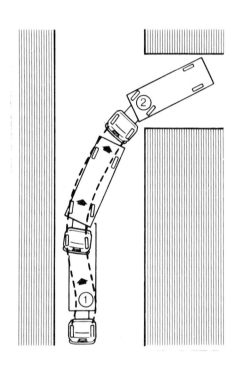

Fig. 7(a)

LEFT-HAND REVERSE OF ARTICULATED VEHICLE

If this manoeuvre cannot be carried out with assistance, the vehicle should be suitably positioned before commencing the reverse. This positioning should allow the driver a clear near-side view and the trailer will commence the reverse in the correct line as shown. *Broad arrows* indicate direction of travel.

(a) Reverse the trailer as close as possible to point (2), "swinging" the steering right and left so that a maximum travel is made and occasionally glancing into offside mirror.

Fig. 7(b) and (c)

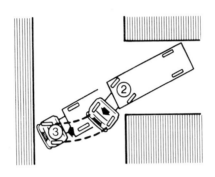

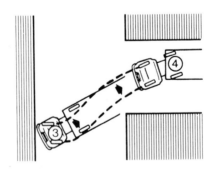

Fig.7(b) and (c)

(b) Drive forward to point (3), quickly "swinging" the steering right and then left to straighten-up the vehicle.

(c) Reverse in a straight line to final position (4).

If during the manoeuvre satisfactory rear view is lost through either mirror, stop, pull forward, reposition the vehicle and resume reverse.

Fig. 8(a)

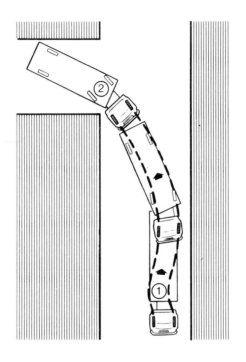

148

Fig.8(a)

RIGHT-HAND REVERSE OF ARTICULATED VEHICLE

Position vehicle as illustrated — as far away as possible from the offside. Look into offside and nearside mirrors and if convenient commence reverse.

(a) Reverse vehicle slowly as indicated by *broad arrows* to point (2), slightly "swinging" steering left and right as indicated by broken line. During the manoeuvre, glance occasionally in the nearside mirror and at the rear tractor wheels.

Fig. 8(b) and (c)

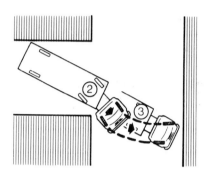

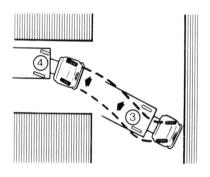

150

Fig.8(b) and (c)

(b) Drive forward to point (3), quickly "swinging" the steering left and then right to straighten up the vehicle.

(c) Glance into mirrors and then reverse vehicle in a straight line to final position (4).

If during the course of the manoeuvre safisfactory rear view is lost through nearside mirror, or if the trailer is incorrectly positioned — stop, pull forward, reposition vehicle and resume reverse.

DRIVING ON MOTORWAYS

Motorways are designed for the purpose of permitting motor vehicles to travel at speed with safety, provided that the rules and regulations laid down are strictly obeyed.

Maximum safety will not be assured unless drivers using motorways are experienced in road procedure and lane drill.

Drivers must also be adept in handling vehicles at speed under prevailing conditions, which include "night driving". Treat the following as a code of practice.

1. Observation drill.

2. Mirror drill.

3. Direction indicator drill.

4. Lights drill.

Rules

A driver must not:

    (a) drive anywhere but on the carriageway

    (b) stop on the carriageway

    (c) reverse on the carriageway

    (d) stop on the central reservation

    (e) stop on verges or hard shoulder, except in case of breakdown, accident or other emergency

    (f) walk on the carriageway or central reservation, except in an emergency

    (g) make a "U-turn"

    (h) use the outside lane of a motorway having three or more lanes when driving
      (i) a goods vehicle exceeding 7.5 tonnes maximum laden weight (2540kg unladen weight);
     (ii) a passenger vehicle exceeding 12m in overall length;
    (iii) a motor vehicle drawing a trailer

(iv) a heavy motor car exceeding 2540kg unladen weight (other than a passenger vehicle not exceeding 12m in overall length), motor tractor, light or heavy locomotive.

(i) disobey remote control signals, such as warning signals — Lane Closed, Maximum Advised Speed, and all other flashing amber light signals

(j) leave the motorway by an entry road.

Conduct on motorways

1. When joining a motorway (other than at its start) the approach will be from a road on the left (slip road). Give way to traffic already on the motorway, watch for a safe gap in the traffic inside lane, then accelerate so that the vehicle is travelling at roughly the same speed as the traffic on it.

2. Drive at a steady speed within the limits of the vehicle. On wet or icy roads, or in fog keep the speed down.

3. Driving for long distances can cause drowsiness. To help prevent this make sure there is a flow of fresh air in the vehicle, suck sweets or turn off at an exit or, if nearby, pull into a service area.

4. Exercise caution and drive well within the limits.

5. Know the braking and stopping distances (see *Highway Code*).

6. Extend courtesy to other road users.

7. Do not "hog" the second or centre lanes.

8. Remember lane discipline:
   (a) nearside lane for *slow moving traffic*
   (b) centre lane for *fast moving traffic*
   (c) outside lane for *fast overtaking traffic* (except heavy goods vehicles).

Car telephones

A driver should **not** stop his vehicle on the hard shoulder of a motorway to make or receive a call, no matter how urgent. (*Highway Code*)

Motorway signals

Matrix signals are used on many stretches of motorway and these are usually positioned at two mile intervals on the central reservation and apply to all lanes. On some very busy stretches overhead gantry signals are used.

When the road ahead is clear the signals are blank but in dangerous conditions amber lights flash and the central panel of the signal will indicate either in figures (which means a temporary speed limit) or symbols (arrows, etc) that a change of lane is necessary, or that the driver must leave the motorway at the next exit, due to an obstruction ahead.

The signals on overhead gantries, which are positioned over each lane, may also show a flashing red light with a red "**X**" sign which means that the vehicle must not **continue beyond the signal in that lane**. Similarly, if red lights flash on a slip road it must not be entered.

All signals should be obeyed since they are there to warn against danger ahead even though it may not be visible.

Driving in fog

Before starting any journey in foggy conditions drivers should:

1. Check that all lights and reflective markings are clean and that lights and indicators are working properly.

2. Clean the windscreen and windows and keep them clean by using wipers, windscreen washer and demister.

   (a) A proper speed, safe separation distance and the maintaining of a safe level of speed are essential.

   (b) For driving in fog there is an advisory speed of 30 mph.

   (c) Fog affects judgement of speed and a driver can easily find himself speeding up without realising it.

   (d) Fog makes tail-lights seem further away than they really are.

   (e) Drivers should know the stopping distances of their vehicles and allow for these.

   (f) Drivers should use **headlights** or front **fog lights** (if fitted) and **rear fog lights**.

Roadworks

Roadworks can be dangerous because in most instances lanes are cordoned off thus reducing the carriageway down to two or even one lane.

Reduced speed limits are also imposed and if the limit shown (usually 50) is on a white background enclosed in a red circle this is the **mandatory** limit and should not be exceeded. Also, heavy vehicles should keep in the near side lane.

Video monitors may be operating at road works to allow the authorities to check on traffic flows — these will also show up any infringements such as speeding etc, which could result in drivers facing prosecution.

Speed limits

Speed limits are given in detail on pages 78–80.

Prohibitions

Among the vehicles that may **not** use motorways are:

Vehicles driven by learner drivers

Pedestrian-controlled vehicles

Animal-drawn vehicles

Agricultural tractors, etc taxed at reduced rate

Engineering plant

Vehicles normally subject to 20 mph speed limit.

Abnormal loads

Drivers moving heavy and abnormal loads over motorways must schedule their journeys to allow plenty of time to reach a parking area off the motorway.

These loads may only be parked in motorway service areas for normal breaks. Overnight parking is not permitted.

Breakdowns

1. If the vehicle breaks down get it as far left of the hard shoulder as possible. Turn on hazard warning lights. If the vehicle breaks down in a contra-flow system turn on hazard warning lights. Take extreme care before getting out of the

vehicle. Do not walk on the carriageway in use if help has to be summoned.

2. If help is needed, use the emergency telephone giving an appropriate description of the vehicle and position. From the information in the "documents" carried give details of equipment, components or tyres, etc, which may assist the police in correctly advising the breakdown services of the requirements.

3. The driver should not wander away from the vehicle as the emergency control cannot call back, so if there is any undue delay a further call should be made to the emergency services.

Condition of vehicles

Vehicle roadworthiness is essential for long journeys and when travelling at speed.

Particular efficiency is required on brakes, steering, batteries and lights, tyres and direction indicators.

Make sure that the following are checked and are in good order, as so many breakdowns and accidents are caused by the neglect of them.

(1) Oil and water levels.

(2) Fuel.

(3) Fan belt (and spare).

(4) Brakes.

(5) Tyres (condition and inflation pressures), spare wheel and jack.

(6) Driving mirrors, windscreen wipers and washers.

(7) Lights and reflectors.

(8) Steering.

Ensure that suitable mudflaps are fitted to commercial vehicles and also that spray guards (required on heavier vehicles) are in good condition in order to prevent water spray being thrown up. Spray and muck from commercial and passenger vehicles when travelling at speed is a considerable hazard to overtaking motorists.

PART THREE

IN TRANSIT AND OFF THE ROAD

LOADING REGULATIONS

Under current legislation there are two sets of regulations affecting the weights and loads that may be carried on vehicles and these are:

1. Maximum axle weights — as laid down by the Road Vehicles (Construction and Use) Regulations.

2. The plated weights or maximum gross vehicle weights — as laid down by the Motor Vehicles (Plating and Testing) Regulations.

The former cover the heaviest weights for various vehicles with different arrangements of axles.

The latter cover the heaviest weights for individual vehicles and must be shown on the vehicle's plate.

In some cases the weights will be the same as those under the construction and use regulations. Where these differ, compliance with the lower weight is required by law.

It is an offence to exceed the weights shown on the DTp or the manufacturer's plate.

Safe loading, distribution and vehicle suitability

1. The weight, packing and distribution of the load must be such that no danger or nuisance is likely to be caused to persons, vehicle or trailer on the road.

2. The load must be evenly distributed on the vehicle or trailer body (this also applies to the loading of containers). A load may be under the gross limit but it does not necessarily mean that the axle weights are not being infringed. This

situation can arise at the time of loading, or by change of load distribution, when individual deliveries are made.

3. A vehicle or trailer should not be used if it is unsuitable for safe loading.

Weighing of vehicles

The Road Traffic Act 1974 makes it a specific offence to obstruct an authorised person or authorised police constable from requiring a motor vehicle to be weighed. The authorised person can instruct the driver to proceed to a weighbridge, including a weighbridge on harbour land, if necessary. He can further require the driver to drive the vehicle, *or drive it himself*, in a particular manner for weighing purposes and he cannot be held liable for any damage or loss of the vehicle, trailer or load provided his actions were reasonable.

If the vehicle is found to be loaded within its limits a certificate will be issued, however, where it is overloaded a GV160 will be issued and the vehicle must be off-loaded to the required limits before it can proceed.

Both the driver and the owner of the vehicle can be prosecuted for an overloading offence.

Dynamic axle weighing machines

The use of dynamic axle weighing machines is allowed for ascertaining the weights transmitted to the road surface of the wheel of each axle of a vehicle and/or trailer and an authorised person can require the driver to drive the vehicle across the weighing platform of the machine for this purpose.

The limits of measured accuracy allowed for the machine is plus or minus 150kg multiplied by the number of axles.

A Certificate of Weight in the prescribed form, is issued on completion of the operation.

Note: an "authorised person" is a certifying officer, goods vehicle examiner, trading standards officer or a specially authorised police constable.

Self weigh facilities at enforcement check sites

The Department of Transport has provided self weighing facilities at certain locations, for drivers to check their vehicles to ensure that they are not overloaded. The facilities are at the Department's enforcement check sites and may be used at any time when they are not being operated for enforcement purposes. No appointment is necessary. The facilities are available 24 hours a day, seven days a week and are free of charge.

A list of weighbridge sites operated by the Department in Great Britain is given on pages 225–228.

Load dimensions

Width: Loads must not project laterally (across the vehicle) more than 305mm on either side but the maximum width of vehicle and load must not exceed **2.9m.**

Length: Department of Transport permission is required for the movement of a load in excess of 27.4m.

The police must be notified for the movement of road trains in excess of 25.9m. Also for an articulated vehicle and load in excess of 18.3m (semi-trailer and load) and articulated vehicle specially built for the carriage of abnormally long loads.

Note: in Central London, police permission is required for the movement between 10.00 hours and 19.00 hours on weekdays of loads exceeding 10.98m in length or 1¾ times the length of the carrying vehicle; also if loads **project** more than 2.6m to the rear.

Projecting loads

These are measured from the foremost or rearmost part of the vehicle, according to which end the projection applies and are regulated as follows:

(a) if a load projects more than 1m to the *rear* it must be made clearly visible with a coloured marker, such as rag or fluorescent material

(b) if a load projects more than 2m to the *front* it must be fitted with a special marker board and an attendent carried

(c) if a load projects more than 2m to the *rear* a marker board must be fitted

(d) if a load projects more than 3.05m to the *front* or *rear* the projection must be fitted with a marker board and a second person in addition to the driver must be in attendance. Prior notice must be given to the police.

Additional side marker boards are required for any forward projection exceeding 4.5m, or any rearward projection exceeding 5m, in which case the marker boards must be fitted within 2.5m and 3.5m respectively of the *normal* marker boards.

Projection marker boards

Diagram of end projection surface

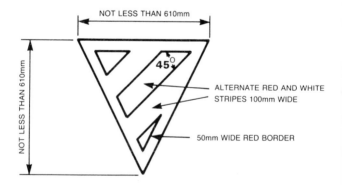

NOT LESS THAN 610mm

NOT LESS THAN 610mm

45°

ALTERNATE RED AND WHITE STRIPES 100mm WIDE

50mm WIDE RED BORDER

Diagram of side projection surface

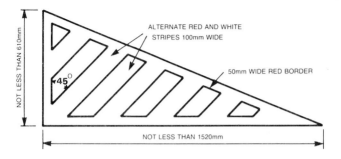

All marker boards must be adequately illuminated at night. (See also page 87.)

Note: a rear reflective marker may be fitted to end projections including abnormal indivisible loads carried on Special Type vehicles, instead of end marker boards and this is especially required where the load being carried obscures the reflective markings fixed to the rear of the vehicle.

PARKING, LOADING AND UNLOADING

A commercial vehicle driver has much to contend with, in complying with the many rules controlling stopping, parking and the loading and unloading of goods.

Prohibition signs used for controlling goods vehicles

Signs erected by local authorities may either ban or restrict the entry of goods vehicles into controlled areas of towns and villages. In certain cases the ban may be for less than 24 hours' duration when access for loading and unloading is allowed. Where prohibition is in force for certain hours of the day this is indicated on the sign.

Signs prohibiting the entry of goods vehicles consist of red circles enclosing black lettering on white ground.

Vehicle prohibited where any axle exceeds the weight indicated (in tonnes)

Vehicle with load exceeding weight indicated (in tonnes) prohibited.

Vehicle exceeding the maximum gross weight indicated (in tonnes). (Permitted variant 16.5 tonnes.*)

Signs similar to the above also indicate height, length or width restrictions on vehicles.

* with the increase in the legal gross weight of two axled rigid vehicles to 17t, local authorities are having to change existing signs. However, until signs showing 17ᵀ are erected vehicles of that weight should not enter the prohibited zone as technically they are breaking the law. Enquiries should be made of the local authority concerned in such matters.

Signs limiting access for loading/unloading

(a)

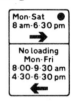

(b)

These signs show hours during which waiting by goods vehicles is prohibited except for loading and unloading (permitted variant 7.5 for 5 on symbol (a)).

Some old style signs showing unladen weight in tons are still in existence as are also those showing measurements in feet and inches but these are gradually being replaced with the new signs.

Parking restrictions

1. It is an offence to leave a vehicle unattended without stopping the engine and securely applying the handbrake.

2. A vehicle and trailer must not be left on the road in such a position as to cause an obstruction.

3. A trailer must not be left on a road detached from the towing vehicle unless the brake is set on at least one wheel or it is secured by a chain, chock or other efficient device to prevent the wheel from moving.

4. Vehicles must not be parked opposite another vehicle or road island.

5. Vehicles must not be parked in a dangerous position, ie on a bridge, on a bend, within the studs of a pedestrian crossing, double white lines and clearways.

It is an offence to park a motor vehicle wholly or partly:

   (a) on the verge of an urban road

   (b) on the footway of an urban road

   (c) on the central reservation of an urban road.

It can be a defence to show that the vehicle was parked with permission given by a police constable in uniform, or in an emergency, or for the purposes of loading or unloading where it would have been unsatisfactory to park elsewhere than on the verge or footpath and the vehicle was not left unattended whilst parked.

Loading and unloading hours

These are shown by a short yellow line 1 foot long painted on the kerb and indicate the following:

   (a) *single marks* at *intervals:* Loading ban at peak hours (am and pm marked on lamp-post)

   (b) *double marks* at *intervals:* Loading ban throughout the day, eg 8.00 am to 6.30 pm

   (c) *treble marks* at *intervals:* Loading bans for more than the working day, eg 8.00 am to midnight.

Notes:

1. Where it is essential to make a delivery or collection at a banned kerb, prior permission from the police should be obtained.

2. Any exemption from loading and unloading does not permit waiting for other purposes.

No waiting and parking

This is indicated by yellow lines painted in the gutter and they do not prevent loading and unloading.

There are three types of yellow lines:

(a) the dotted line which indicates "no waiting" for part of the day

(b) the solid yellow line which indicates "no waiting" for the normal working day

(c) the double yellow line which indicates "no waiting" for more than the working day.

Similarly to the kerb signs, the times of these bans will be shown on the lamp-post signs.

Notes:

1. Drivers may only stop to load and unload in a "no waiting" street and not for any other purpose.

2. Drivers may only stop in the main road if there is no rear or side access which can be used for loading or unloading.

3. Drivers may stop only for the period allowed for unloading (normally 20 minutes). If it is not possible to "put down" or "pick up" within that time prior permission should be obtained from the police for an extension of time.

4. A police officer has the right to move vehicles on.

Priority route network

A new scheme for a priority route network has recently been introduced and is operating (at the moment) in a part of London on an experimental basis. Known as the "Red Route" double red painted lines on roads mean that vehicles are prohibited from stopping at any time and on roads painted with single red lines stopping for loading and unloading is only permitted at certain times, usually outside the working day.

Breakdown and removal of vehicles

1. If a vehicle breaks down in a prohibited street and must be left in order to obtain assistance, the police or traffic wardens should be notified. Hazard warning lights should be switched on.

2. The police are empowered to remove any vehicle which is causing an obstruction, contravening waiting, loading, unloading restrictions or left in a dangerous position.

Parking meters

Parking meters are included with the kerb marking signs which are displayed on discs to indicate the "controlled zone".

Vacant parking meter bays may normally be used for up to 20 minutes without charge, for loading and unloading.

Double parking alongside parking bays or loading gaps which are already occupied is prohibited.

Traffic wardens

Traffic wardens are empowered to enforce the law in connection with the following offences:

(a) compulsory lights or reflectors

(b) waiting, parking, loading or obstruction and in connection with parking meters by use of the fixed penalty system.

Fixed penalty system

Fixed fines can be imposed without the case being heard in court and this system operates in towns and cities throughout the country.

Under this system tickets may be issued by traffic wardens for offences as outlined above and also for — parking at night without obligatory lights or reflectors; not showing a current excise licence.

The Road Traffic Regulation Act 1984 provides for registered owners of motor vehicles to carry the ultimate responsibility for the payment of certain *fixed penalty* and *excess* parking charges when these have not been settled within the time allowed, ie 28 days. The liabilities relate to fixed penalties of the following:

(a) parking a vehicle on a road during the hours of darkness without lights or reflectors required by law

(b) contravention of waiting, parking, loading and unloading restrictions

(c) non-payment of a parking meter charge

(d) keeping a vehicle on a public road without a current licence.

Owner liability also extends to excess charges.

Exceptions to these requirements are:

(1) The registered owner shall not be deemed to be the driver if it is proved that at the relevant time the vehicle was in the possession of some other person without the owner's consent.

(2) In the case of hired vehicles (hired for less than six months) the payment of the relevant charges rests with the hirer and not the registered owner.

Whilst the ultimate responsibility for the settlement of unpaid charges rests with the owner, this in no way absolves the actual driver.

The Road Traffic Offenders Act 1988 schedule 3 lists the offences for which fixed penalties can be issued which are as follows —

1. Leaving a vehicle parked at night without lights or reflectors.

2. Waiting, parking, loading or unloading.

3. Controlled parking zone regulations.

4. Failure to display a current excise licence disc.

5. Making "U" turns in unauthorised places.

6. Lighting offences by moving vehicles.

7. Banned right turns and driving the wrong way in a one-way street.

8. Contravening a traffic regulation order.

9. Breach of experimental traffic order.

10. Breach of experimental traffic scheme regulation in Greater London.

11. Using a vehicle in contravention of a temporary prohibition or restriction of traffic on a road, ie where a road is being repaired, etc.

12. Contravening motorway traffic regulations.

13. Driving a vehicle in contravention of order prohibiting or restricting driving vehicles on certain classes of roads.

14. Breach of pedestrian crossing regulations*.

15. Contravention of a street playground order*.

16. Breach of a parking place order on a road.

17. Breach of a provision of a parking place designation order and other offences committed in relation to it, except failing to pay an excess charge.

18. Contravening a parking place designation order.

19. Breach of a provision of a parking place designation order.

20. Contravention of minimum speed limits.

21. Speeding†.

22. Driving or keeping a vehicle without displaying registration mark or hackney carriage sign.

23. Driving or keeping a vehicle with registration mark or hackney carriage sign obscured.

24. Failure to comply with traffic directions or signs.

25. Leaving vehicle in a dangerous position.

26. Failing to wear a seat belt.

27. Breach of restrictions on carrying children in the front of vehicles.

28. Driving a vehicle elsewhere than on the road.

29. Parking a vehicle on the path or verge.

30. Breach of construction and use regulations.*

31. Contravention of lighting restrictions on vehicles.

32. Driving without a licence*.

33. Breach of provisional licence conditions†.

34. Failure to stop when required by constable in uniform.

35. Obstruction of highway with vehicle.

* endorsement is obligatory in certain circumstances.
† endorsement is obligatory.

For most of these offences only police officers may issue fixed penalty tickets; traffic wardens continue to deal mainly with parking offences as in the past.

Police officers are still able to warn drivers. In appropriate cases a police officer may issue a fixed penalty ticket or, in more serious cases, prosecute in the normal way. Once a police officer has issued a fixed penalty ticket the driver has 28 days (or as specified in the notice) to pay. The driver still has the option to contest the offence in court and this is explained clearly on the fixed penalty notice. If the driver does not take either course within 28 days the penalty is increased by 50% and enforced by the courts as an unpaid fine. Thus a £16 (non-endorsable) fixed penalty becomes a £24 fine and the £32 (licence endorsable) penalty rises to £48.

The fixed penalty tickets for the less serious non-endorsable offences are usually white.

The endorsable tickets are yellow and attract the higher penalty of £32. Where a police officer has decided to issue a fixed penalty ticket for an endorsable offence he will ask to see the driver's licence so that the existing number of penalty points can be checked. A ticket will be issued and the driver asked to surrender his licence in return for a receipt which will be valid for two months. If the penalty points for the present offence added to those which may already be on the licence total 12 or more — the level for disqualification — a driver will not be issued with a fixed penalty notice but will be reported for prosecution so that he may put forward any reasons in court why he should not be disqualified. A driver who is not carrying his licence will be required to take it to the police station of his choice within seven days. If a driver is ever stopped for an endorsable offence it will therefore be much more convenient if he is carrying his driving licence with him. Penalty points for traffic offences are given on pages 67–68.

Parking on the road at night without lights

The Road Vehicles Lighting Regulations 1989 allow vehicles to be parked on the road at night without lights in the following circumstances:

1. Motor cars, motor cycles, and goods vehicles **not** exceeding 1525kg unladen weight provided that:

   (a) the road is subject to a 30 mph speed limit, or less

   (b) no part of the vehicle is within 10m of a road junction

   (c) the vehicle is parked close to the kerb and parallel to it and, except in the case of one-way streets, has its near-side to the kerb.

   On all other roads the obligatory side and rear lights **must be switched on**.

2. Vehicles parked in an area on part of the highway on which road works are being carried out and which are bounded by amber lamps and other traffic signs (cones, etc) to prevent the vehicle, its load or equipment being a danger to other road users.

Passenger vehicles adapted to carry *eight or more* passengers excluding the driver, goods vehicles exceeding 1525kg unladen weight, and any vehicle to which a trailer is attached, must keep their lights (side lamps) on when parked on the road at night.

When lights are required on a parked vehicle two white lights must be shown at the front and two red lights to the rear.

It is **illegal** to use either a single parking light or a device which switches on only the offside front and rear lamps.

Overnight parking

Many borough councils (especially in the Greater London area) prohibit the parking of commercial vehicles, ie those over 2½ tons unladen weight, in residential streets overnight. The restrictions apply from 18.30 hours to midnight and midnight to 08.00 hours seven days a week. Off street parking is usually available where such bans are in force.

The Greater London area lorry ban

Goods vehicles exceeding 16.5 tonnes maximum gross weight are prohibited from using the majority of roads in the Greater London area during the following times:

(a) Monday to Friday — between midnight and 07.00 hours and 21.00 hours and midnight

(b) Saturdays — between midnight and 07.00 hours and 13.00 hours and midnight

(c) Sundays — at any time

unless they are covered by an exemption permit.

A permit which allows journeys to be made during the prohibited times must be carried on the vehicle and distinguishing plates must be fixed in a conspicuous place, one at the front of the vehicle and the other at the rear. The plates are for ease of identification by the enforcement authorities.

It is an offence to use a vehicle in the prohibited area unless an exemption permit is in force.

VEHICLE MAINTENANCE

The law requires all users of motor vehicles, whether driver, owner-driver or employer, to maintain the vehicles they use to specific standards for the benefit of road and public safety. The requirements cover inspections, tests, checks and the keeping of records to support such action. There are severe penalties for failure to comply with the regulations.

Commercial vehicles above 3.5 tonnes gross laden weight are covered by the Transport Act 1968 (s.6), the Goods Vehicles (Operators' Licences, Qualifications and Fees) Regulations 1984, the Goods Vehicles (Plating and Testing) Regulations 1988 and the Road Traffic Act 1988. Vehicles up to 3.5 tonnes gross laden weight (light vans, passenger vehicles and private cars) public service vehicles, community buses, school buses belonging to a local education authority, taxis and ambulances are covered by the Road Traffic Act 1988, the Motor Vehicles (Construction & Use) Regulations 1986 and the Motor Vehicles (Tests) Regulations 1981.

Items subject to correct maintenance, tests and inspections are: steering; brakes; tyres; windscreen wipers and washers; direction indicators; lighting equipment; noise (check on excess); exhaust system; and seat belts (correct fitting anchorage and the BSI Kite Mark).

Maintenance of tyres

It is illegal to use a tyre which:

(a) is not correctly inflated

(b) has a break in the fabric or a cut in excess of 25mm or 10% of the section width of the tyre, deep enough to reach the ply or cord

(c) has a lump, bulge or tear caused by separation, etc

(d) is the wrong size or type for the vehicle's use

(e) has any portion of the ply or cord exposed

(f) has the base of any groove which showed in the original tread pattern of the tyre not clearly visible

(g) either (i) the grooves of the tread pattern do not have a depth of at least 1mm* throughout a continuous band measuring at least ¾ of the breadth of tread round the entire outer circumference of the tyre, or (ii) where the original tread pattern did not extend beyond ¾ of the breadth of the tread, the base of any groove which

* from 1.1.92 this is increased to 1.6mm for cars, light vans and light trailers up to 3500kg maximum gross weight.

showed in the tyre's original tread pattern does not
have a depth of at least 1mm.

Correct pressures must be maintained and should always be
taken when the tyres are cold. They should be checked daily
and a spare carried which must also be maintained in good
order and at the correct pressure.

Extending tyre life

Tyres are one of the most important safety factors on a motor
vehicle and the rate of road accidents through tyre failure is
still very high. Tyre maintenance costs can amount to up to
25% of total maintenance costs and this fact alone gives some
idea why they should be properly maintained.

Premature tyre wear need not have anything to do with the
tyre itself. For example — brake judder or grate results in
uneven wear and when the tyre laws are taken into account
that can soon mean the end of the useful life of the tyre. If the
toe-in of the front wheels is incorrect, tyres will wear rapidly as
well. Here the wear is on the shoulders and on the edges of the
blocks of the tread and is equally expensive.

Tyres are expensive, therefore everything possible must be
done to extend their lives — and the ways and means in which
vehicles are maintained can have a profound effect on tyre life.
Apart from what has previously been indicated, when it comes
to *routine* maintenance of the tyres, the importance of correct
tyre pressures cannot be overstressed. If tyres are *under-in-
flated*, they will wear excessively on the shoulders and if they
are *over-inflated* the wear takes place on the crown — and the
tyre is more vulnerable to cuts and abrasion.

At the same time, it is important that the pressures in twin
tyres are identical, a difference of 10 psi can result in overloading of the tyres.

A point frequently overlooked is the need for the tyres on
the opposite sides of a driven axle to be of equal diameters or
rolling radii — in other words **do not** put a pair of new tyres on
one side when those on the other side are fairly well worn.

Although the differential unit can accommodate the difference in diameters, it is not designed for continuous operation and so is likely to wear rapidly in such a situation.

Fortunately, punctures do not occur as frequently as they used to and most of them are the result of debris found on sites and poorly kept roads. Frequently tyres pick up pieces of metal or swarf, etc which gets worked into the tyre carcass once the vehicle is on the move.

The practice of thoroughly inspecting the tyres before commencing a run or moving off from a littered site, must become a routine responsibility.

This sort of inspection and check is the job most drivers want to avoid, so it becomes necessary to convince them of the cost and inconvenience caused by having a puncture en route. In terms of productivity, routine checking of tyres pays handsomely, as a puncture on the road does nobody any good, even if the tyre(s) is replaced quickly.

When applied to tyres, routine or preventative maintenance is not just a question of checking the pressures periodically, looking for nails or stones in the tyres or renewing the tyres before the treads reach the minimum legal tread depth. It is also a matter of looking for any signs of uneven wear, ensuring that tyres are properly matched to the axle and to the job and the correctness of steering geometry, wheel balancing and driving techniques.

TESTING AND INSPECTION OF VEHICLES

For the purpose of ensuring that goods and passenger-carrying vehicles are maintained in a "fit and serviceable" condition, tests and inspections can be carried out on the road or on operators' premises by Department of Transport certifying officers, vehicle examiners, or police officers in uniform.

The test, checks and inspections to which the goods vehicle is subject are as follows.

1. **Spot checks** — on the road and on premises. On production of his authority an examiner or certifying officer is empowered to examine a vehicle on the road or on premises. Both are permitted to divert a vehicle for up to five miles (if stopped on the road) to carry out the check. *Failure to comply can result in a heavy fine.*

2. **Inspection of vehicles on premises** — to examine and test brakes, steering, gears, tyres, silencers, noise, lighting equipment and reflectors. Minor items such as those affecting the security of the body, cab and wings (to ensure safety) may also be subject to report on prohibition notices.

3. **Annual tests** — cover both cars and light goods vehicles under one test and medium and heavy goods vehicles under another. Passenger-carrying vehicles, etc must also be tested annually (see below).

   (a) **Light vehicle testing** – Goods vehicles not exceeding 3500kg gross weight, dual-purpose vehicles not exceeding 2030kg unladen weight, motor caravans, and private cars must all be tested annually when three years of age or over.

   (b) **Medium and heavy vehicle testing** — all goods vehicles over 3500kg gross weight, and trailers over 1020kg unladen, (also converter dollies), are subject to an annual test at LGV testing stations for renewal of the Test certificate.

   (c) **Public service vehicles, other large passenger vehicles**, ie vehicles having more than eight seats excluding the driver such as works buses, voluntary sector buses, ambulances and taxis (unless they are tested by a local authority and they issue a test certificate) must all be tested annually from one year old.

The month for testing depends on the vehicle's date of first registration and it is an offence to drive a vehicle without a valid certificate after its due date for testing.

Prohibitions

If, after carrying out a "spot-check" inspection, the examiner considers a goods vehicle unfit for service, he may prohibit its use on the road for the carriage of goods by issuing an immediate prohibition notice on form PG9.

If the vehicle defects do not involve immediate risk to safety the examiner can issue a deferred prohibition notice. Under a deferred prohibition, the continued use of the vehicle is permitted but the defects must be rectified within the period stated on the form PG9 and most certainly within 10 days. The notice may direct that the vehicle must be inspected at a vehicle testing station.

A vehicle issued with a deferred prohibition notice must not be used after the expiration of the period of grace, until the prohibition has been withdrawn.

In the event of a PG9 being issued in respect of the vehicle the facts and the faults must be reported to the employer — it is an offence to drive a motor vehicle under a prohibition notice.

Annual tests

For the benefit of drivers who will no doubt have to take vehicles to testing stations, also owner-drivers who, like the employer, will be totally involved, some further information on plating and testing is given.

1. **Applications** for first tests must be made on the appropriate form (VTG1L for motor vehicles, or VTG2L for trailers and semi-trailers and thereafter on form VTG40L ("L" stands for local) and sent, accompanied by the correct fee (see page 177) to the Department of Transport, Goods Vehicle Licensing Centre, 91-92 The Strand, Swansea. The GVLC will retain the fee and pass the application form to the testing station nominated by the operator who will then notify him of the date and time of the test. The application should be made at least one month before the end of the relevant testing period and one month before the desired date.

2. **Tests** are booked for specific times and the vehicle must be presented at the allocated time.

The test covers about 65 items, which are listed in the testers' manual, and copies of this can be obtained from HM Stationery Office.

Time for the test is about 40 to 45 minutes and if the test is successful a goods vehicle test certificate (Form VTG5) will be issued. If the test is unsuccessful Form VTG4 will be issued but a certificate will not be issued.

3. A Department examiner can refuse to carry out the test for a variety of reasons, including:

   (a) being over 30 minutes late
   (b) failing to produce the appointment card, registration document, plating certificate or other means of the vehicle's first registration
   (c) vehicle not accompanied by a trailer when the appointment card states that a trailer should accompany the vehicle
   (d) no fuel or oil in the vehicle
   (e) vehicle dirty or in a dangerous condition
   (f) serial or chassis number, as shown in the registration document, missing
   (g) vehicle breaks down during test
   (h) vehicle not loaded in accordance with instructions on test appointment card
   (i) vehicle not displaying its Ministry plate.

The driver should be given the "booking card" to hand in at test centre office on arrival.

As the test is in four stages, the driver will be asked to drive the vehicle from one stage to another and, at the same time, operate the various controls.

Examiners are not required to dismantle parts or equipment of vehicles, therefore, if only minor faults are found the driver, or the mechanic if he accompanies the driver, will be allowed to put them right on the spot and re-submit the vehicle for inspection.

If the faults are more serious then the vehicle will have to be taken away and another test appointment arranged.

Fees

The current fees for testing and plating are :

Motor Vehicles £30.80   *Trailers £18.60*

The "tractor" and "trailer" portions of articulated vehicles are charged separately. There is no additional plating fee.

Re-tests on the day of, or the day after, the original test are free.

Fees for re-tests carried out within 14 days at the same station as the original test are currently £15.60 for motor vehicles and £9.00 for trailers.

Tests can also be carried out at certain test stations on a Saturday and for this there is a supplementary fee of £18.60 for motor vehicles and £11.70 for trailers. The Saturday supplements for re-tests are £9.30 and £5.80 respectively.

For an examination requested by the operator following alteration of a vehicle the current fee is £12.90 plus £8 supplement if it is conducted on a Saturday.

The fee for the issue of a replacement plate, plating certificate or test certificate is £8.80.

TRADE LICENCES AND TRADE PLATES

Trade licences permit the use on the roads of vehicles which have not been licensed individually but only **one vehicle at a time** may be so used and only for a prescribed purpose.

They are only issued to "motor traders" defined as "manufacturers, repairers, dealers and businesses engaged in the modifying or valeting of mechanically propelled vehicles", and "vehicle testers". A fleet owner who carries out his own repairs is therefore entitled to a trade licence.

Applications for trade licences should be made on Form VE7 to the local Vehicle Registration Office (VRO) in whose area the trader's business premises are situated. They will issue to the holder of a trade licence a set of two number plates (known as "trade plates"). The excise licence is fixed to one of these.

The carriage of goods is not permitted except in certain circumstances, ie demonstration purposes, etc and the only persons to be carried, other than the driver, are a vehicle inspector, a prospective buyer or his agent.

Lost, defaced or destroyed trade licence plates can be replaced at a cost of £11 per set or £6.50 for the plate containing the licence and £4.50 in any other case.

Cost of Licence: currently £85 per annum or £46.75 for six months.

Penalties for infringement of the regulations are a fine of up to £200 or five times the correct excise duty, whichever is the greater.

RECOVERY VEHICLES

A recovery vehicle is defined as "a vehicle which is either constructed or permanently adapted primarily for the purpose of lifting, towing and transporting a disabled vehicle or for any one or more of these purposes" and since January 1988 such vehicles have been subject to a separate category insofar as excise licensing is concerned and chargeable with duty at (currently) £75 per annum, or £41.25 per six months.

If a vehicle is so licensed it is restricted in use to:
- (a) the recovery of a broken down vehicle
- (b) the removal of a broken down vehicle from the place where it broke down to premises for repair or for scrapping
- (c) removing a broken down vehicle from premises to which it had been taken for repair to other premises for repair or scrapping, and
- (d) carrying only fuel and other liquid required for the propulsion of the vehicle and tools and other articles required for the operation of or in connection with apparatus designed to lift, tow or transport a disabled vehicle.

Persons or goods may be carried in the recovery vehicle if they were previously in the broken down vehicle immediately prior to its breaking down in circumstances under items (a) and (b) above. They may also be carried, together with their personal effects from the premises at which the broken down vehicle is to be repaired or scrapped, to their original intended destination.

Also, again in circumstances under items (a) and (b) above, a recovery vehicle may be used

(i) for the repair of a broken down vehicle either at the site of the breakdown or at the place to which it had been moved in the interests of safety, or

(ii) for towing or carrying one trailer which had previously been towed or carried by the vehicle immediately prior to its breaking down.

A vehicle ceases to be classed as a recovery vehicle if it is used for any purposes other than those described above.

An operator still has the choice of taxing a recovery vehicle at the standard rate of duty based on the vehicle's gross weight in which case there are no restrictions on its use.

Application for a recovery vehicle licence has to be made to a Vehicle Registration Office (VRO).

INSURANCE

Compulsory cover

It is legally necessary to have insurance cover in accordance with the Traffic Acts and full third party insurance provides cover for personal injury or property damage sustained by third parties. Upon the issue of a third party policy, a certificate of insurance is also issued, which confirms that the cover conforms to the Acts and this certificate must be produced upon request from a police officer, or within seven days at any police station.

Policies normally extend to cover liability arising during loading and unloading of a vehicle but excluding liability during loading and unloading beyond the carriageway or thoroughfare by any person other than the driver or attendant of such a vehicle.

A third party insurance policy provides cover in respect of compensation for injury caused to another and also the cost of any emergency medical treatment resulting from an accident. Also included is legal liability for claims for damage to the property of third parties.

The Road Traffic Act 1988 requires that users of motor vehicles are covered against any liability which may occur in respect of death or personal injury to their passengers in the use of the vehicle on the road. All passengers must be covered and no "own risks" agreements are allowed.

If required, a third party policy can be extended to include risks of fire and theft of the insured vehicle. Should insurance be required to cover additional damage to the vehicle, it is necessary to take out a "comprehensive policy" which, apart from covering accidental damage, also embraces third party risks, fire and theft.

Continental cover

It is necessary to advise the insurers when Continental cover is required and most insurers will extend policies for use on the Continent upon payment of an additional premium and they will issue an International Motor Insurance Card, commonly known as a "Green Card".

Third party insurance is compulsory in most Continental countries and the Green Card is accepted by all the Continental countries subscribing to the Green Card Scheme as evidence that the vehicle is insured in accordance with their regulations for third party insurance. The additional premium charged for Continental use is usually calculated at a set amount per week and therefore the operator should ensure that he only arranges cover for the actual period of Continental use involved.

EC requirements

All British motor insurance policies must include cover against those liabilities which are compulsorily insurable in all other Member States of the European Community and non-EC countries, Austria, Czechoslovakia, Finland, Hungary, Norway, Sweden and Switzerland. It is an offence to use a vehicle or trailer that is not so insured even though it may never leave Great Britain.

Most insurance companies now automatically give "EC Territorial Limits" in respect of compulsory insurance requirements for each of the member states. In those cases while it is still necessary to advise insurers, it is not strictly necessary to have a Green Card. However, if Comprehensive cover is required for foreign use, it is recommended that the policy be extended to provide full comprehensive cover for all the countries to be visited, in which case a Green Card will normally be issued. For journeys to Spain a Bail Bond is also advisable.

It is also important to ensure that the vehicle is covered while being carried by sea and that the driver is insured whilst abroad especially for medical and repatriation expenses.

It is also an offence for a person to use, in a Member State, or any of the other countries mentioned above, a vehicle which, though exempted from insurance in this country, does not have a policy covering the risks required to be covered by the laws of the Member State or other country concerned. Vehicles exempt from insurance in this country include those whose owners have deposited cash or securities to the value of £15,000 with the Supreme Court.

The Regulations also provide for the checking at points of entry of insurance documents for all vehicles registered in countries not covered by these regulations and failure to provide evidence of proper insurance can result in the vehicle being detained and prevented from using the roads.

Notwithstanding the above comments hauliers operating from the United Kingdom **should continue** to notify their insurers in advance of all intended journeys abroad and should see that they are adequately covered against all liabilities. Where the "Green Card" is issued it should accompany the vehicle. Where a trailer is used this should be specified separately on the Green Card.

Notes:

1. Always give insurers ample notice when new or additional cover is required. The correct insurance cover is as important as correct maintenance for safety with motor vehicle operations.

2. Policies are usually invalidated if the vehicles insured are not maintained in a safe and roadworthy condition.

Goods in transit insurance

This insurance cover mainly concerns the operator (the employer) and owner-drivers but in view of its importance and involvement with Continental operations where, in many cases, the driver is the sole representative, some points of procedure are worth mentioning.

A goods in transit insurance policy should always be effected for the transporting of goods.

The operator must ensure that the cover he arranges indemnifies him fully in accordance with the conditions under which he carries goods for his clients and therefore the insurers must be advised of the conditions. These conditions of carriage are usually those of the Road Haulage Association and should be brought to the notice of every client.

Some clients may request special or wider insurance cover than that offered by the carrier. Where this arises, the carrier must advise his insurers to ensure that they will extend the policy to meet the client's additional requirements.

Many insurers now insert special clauses in their policies for the further safeguard and security of goods in transit and the most usual of these are:

1. **Immobiliser clause** requires motor vehicles to be fitted with an approved anti-theft device which is put into effective operation *at all times* when the vehicle is loaded and left unattended.

2. **Night risk clause** requires that vehicles left loaded overnight must not be left unattended unless *locked* and *immobilised* in accordance with any such provision under the policy and

also that they are either left in a building or yard which is also securely closed and locked, or in an official vehicle park covered by attendants.

Further reference to the security of vehicles and loads will be covered under the heading in the following section.

VEHICLE SECURITY

Vehicle and load security is one of the most important problems with which operators and drivers have to contend.

Whatever the precautions taken, and there are various effective measures which are being put to use, it is the driver who is responsible for their effectiveness.

The theft of vehicles, equipment and loads is now very big business and, to some extent, the development of this has been due to the lack of the necessary precautions being applied, or through driver negligence.

Vehicle protection

Of all the offences coming under the heading of "simple theft", that of property from unattended vehicles represents the biggest single problem to the police, as the loss of a commercial vehicle load alone can amount to many thousands of pounds. It is, therefore, quite understandable why the insurance companies insist on goods vehicles being fitted with anti-theft devices.

Immobilisers for vehicle protection are of two main varieties — electrical and mechanical.

Electrical immobilisers work on the alarm system, but cut off the ignition, starter motor, or fuel supply. Operation is usually by a key or a combination lock mechanism, set after the cab has been vacated.

Mechanical immobilisers are operated by applying physical methods in the form of locks upon gear shifts, brakes or parts of the engine and steering mechanism. There are also other complex methods which involve the transmission and the differential or the hydraulic braking system.

Alarm warning systems are also used as an additional form of vehicle security and can be installed separately or incorporated with the immobiliser system. Most alarm systems are electrically operated, either by use of the existing horn of the vehicle or one specially fitted with a siren of distinctive note.

Trailer protection

The protection and security of trailers presents a problem as it is not possible for the immobilising devices to function when the motive unit is separated from the trailer. Various methods of securing trailers are being used, such as the securing of brakes, suspensions and turntables with chains and padlocks but owing to the possibility of thieves using hacksaws, extra caution has to be taken in the fitting of these locks and chains.

The most satisfactory method currently used by operators is the fitting of a pivoted steel clamp around the trailer kingpin. This clamp must also be fitted with a hacksaw-proof padlock. Remember to use a lock which will be unsuitable to hacksaw blades and sufficiently close shackled to prevent it being easily forced.

Most experienced commercial drivers will already have had experience with the various security methods but for newcomers to the professional ranks it is as well to have some idea of the various applications, particularly in the attention to be paid to fitting, removal, stowage and the care and security of keys.

Remember! The driver who secures a particular trailer may not be the one to unlock it!

Load Security

Compared with vehicle protection, the security of loads is a much more difficult problem, although in part, vehicle protection is load protection.

Open platform trucks and trailers present the most difficult problem owing to their vulnerability to theft of load or part loads. Loads carried on these vehicles have to be sheeted-down, but the security of the sheeting-down will vary according to whether the driver is on distribution with multiple drops or a distance journey or trunk service.

It is common practice to steal from loads parked overnight at transport cafes by undoing ropes on and around the sheeting. The easiest way to prevent this is for the vehicle to be parked in a well-lit or guarded car park. Also, when pulling in at cafes, particular care must be taken when parking, so that the vehicle may be left in a reasonably conspicuous position to discourage any attempt to steal the load.

With box-body vehicles, trailers and containers there is no difficulty in protecting the loads from theft as these can be suitably wired and installed with an alarm system. Rear doors can be fitted with close-shackled padlocks.

Advice to drivers

1. Do not park in quiet laybys.
2. Do not visit transport cafes where there are recurrent incidents of theft.
3. Use guarded or well-lit car parks for overnight parking.
4. Do not leave vehicles in back streets near to lodgings for personal convenience.
5. When in doubt notify the police of the presence of the load.
6. Check immobilisers, alarms and locks before leaving the vehicle for the night.
7. Do not carry casual passengers.
8. A driver should view with suspicion any moving and flashing lights to indicate faults with his vehicle.
9. Report to the police and the employer any approaches from strangers to steal the load.

The essential requirements of a thief when stealing vehicles and/or loads are many and well planned but the most important, which must be denied him by the driver are:

(a) the ability to remove the vehicle and/or its load

(b) the opportunity to do so

(c) sufficient time to carry out the theft without interference or attracting attention.

The driver is all important. His integrity is worth any amount of alarms and immobilisers, which are useless without his co-operation. With no special equipment there is much that he can do as an individual but he should have more than the cab door locks to assist him.

ATTENDANTS

An attendant is required on a heavy locomotive drawing a trailer(s) and carrying an abnormal and indivisible load (as defined by the Motor Vehicle (Authorisation of Special Types) General Order 1979). An attendant is also required in certain circumstances when a standard vehicle carries a projecting load.

CARRIAGE OF FOOD

Food means food intended for sale or sold for human consumption, including drink, and "handling" includes transport.

The special requirements which apply in the case of vehicles used for the carriage or sale of food and drink are contained in:

- Food Hygiene (Market, Stalls and Delivery Vehicles) Regulations 1966
- Food Hygiene (Scotland) Amendment Regulations 1966
- Food Hygiene (Docks, Carriers, etc) Regulations 1966
- Food Hygiene (Amendment) Regulations 1990

Cleanliness and handling

Food delivery vehicles and mobile shops must be constructed so that the food is not exposed to risk of contamination.

Drivers and assistants who handle food must:

(a) wear clean clothing and refrain from smoking

(b) keep food clean and free from contamination and suitably covered during sale and delivery

(c) cover cuts with a waterproof dressing.

The employer is responsible for ensuring that suitable washing facilities and first-aid equipment are available and it is the driver's duty to make use of these facilities as required for the benefit of hygiene.

Live animals and poultry must not come into contact with meat or fish.

Delivery vehicles exceeding 7.5 tonnes gross weight carrying certain types of "relevant food" products must be able to maintain the temperature of the food at or below specified temperatures ie 8°C or at or above 63°C (from 1.4.93 the lower temperature will be either 5°C or 8°C depending on the type of food being carried).

From 1.4.92 goods vehicles up to 7.5 tonnes gross weight used for local deliveries must also be capable of maintaining temperatures at 5°C or at or above 63°C. Certain exceptions apply depending on the length of time beween preparation and sale of the food.

Garaging
Mobile shops or food delivery vehicles may not be garaged with food inside unless the food can be kept clean.

CARRIAGE OF MEAT

The requirements relating to the carriage of meat are covered by the Food Hygiene (General) Regulations 1960.

Cleanliness and handling
Drivers and their mates when employed by regular meat carriers and by meat traders must observe strict cleanliness and hygiene precautions, which are:

(a) wear clean and washable overalls

(b) keep meat clean and free from contamination

(c) cover cuts with a waterproof dressing.

Although it is the employer's responsibility to ensure that the vehicles carrying meat are kept thoroughly clean, drivers and mates must, during the course of their duties, see that vehicles are kept clean and any wooden floors must be fitted with movable duckboards which, together with any other equipment, must be kept clean.

Offal detached from carcasses must be carried in separate impervious containers.

CARRIAGE OF LIVE ANIMALS

The utmost care and hygiene must be observed when transporting live animals and it is an offence to cause unnecessary suffering to any animal by carrying it in a road vehicle when the animal is not in a fit condition. This does not apply if, of course, the vehicle in which the animal is carried is being correctly used as an ambulance.

The regulations governing the transporting, handling and care of live animals are:

- The Movement and Sale of Pigs Order 1975 and Amendment Order 1975
- The Transit of Animals (Road and Rail) Order 1975.

Animals may only be carried in road vehicles which have a substantial roof and sides which protect from the weather without impeding ventilation.

Inspection of the interior must be possible from the outside, the floor and tailboard or loading ramp must be fitted with battens and barriers must be provided to minimise injury to the animals.

The floor must be covered with an adequate amount of bedding material.

The animals must be supplied with food and water at intervals of not longer than 12 hours except that where a journey is completed within 15 hours it is sufficient if they are fed immediately on arrival at destination.

If pigs or sheep are carried in the same vehicle, they must be separated from calves by an adequate barrier.

Pigs

Drivers and owner drivers should obtain a copy of The Movement and Sale of Pigs Order 1975 (SI 1975 No. 203) and Amendment Orders 1975 (SI 1975 No. 346) and 1987 (SI 1987

No. 233) as restrictions are laid down on the use of road vehicles for the carrying of pigs.

Regulations 1-7 of the main order deal with the restrictions on the movement of pigs from certain premises, etc; reg. 8 requires that a road vehicle must not be used for carrying pigs unless it has been cleansed and disinfected. Within 24 hours of carrying pigs and in any case before it is used for carrying any other animal or thing it must be cleaned and thoroughly disinfected.

It is an offence to carry other animals in a vehicle used for transporting pigs unless the cleansing operation has been carried out.

Horses
Horses must be transported in specially designed and constructed vehicles of specific dimensions.

Heavy draught horses must face either the front or the rear of the vehicle. Horses carried lengthwise must be tied with a light headrope.

Small ponies, asses, mules and jennets and a mare with foal at foot may be carried in the same vehicle when separated by a suitable partition.

Hygiene of vehicles and equipment
All dung, fodder, litter, etc, must be removed and the vehicle floor, sides and parts must be thoroughly swept and scraped clean, washed and sprayed with disinfectant after use and before any other horse fodder, etc, is placed in it.

Scrapings, sweepings and other matter removed from vehicles must be burnt at once and removed from all contact with horses.

Feeding and watering
On journeys exceeding 12 hours each animal must be provided with sufficient food and water which must be supplied at intervals of not more than 12 hours during any journey.

Infirm horses
It is an offence to carry any horse which, through infirmity, illness, injury or fatigue would suffer unnecessarily.

Records of movements

The operator is responsible for keeping a record of the movements of animals in any vehicle used regularly for such purpose and this must be available at his place of business.

The driver of the vehicle must carry a record on the vehicle in which must be entered: the time of loading; the time and place of feeding and watering, if any and the time of unloading. The entries must be made at the time the action takes place.

The record must be produced on demand by an inspector or police constable.

A record need not be kept where a vehicle is carrying a horse and the journey is completed in less than three hours.

WELFARE OF LIVE POULTRY

The carriage of live poultry is covered by The Welfare of Poultry (Transport) Order 1988 (S.I. 1988 No. 851). The order also covers movements by rail, sea and air but this summary is confined to transport by road.

"Poultry" means live birds of the following species — domestic fowls, turkeys, geese, ducks, guinea-fowls, pheasants, partridges and quails.

The requirements for carrying are very similar to those applying to animals (see page 188) in that the birds must not be subject to any unnecessary suffering or injury whilst in transit. They must be protected from the weather and not exposed to temperature fluctuations, noise or vibration. Adequate supplies of food and water must be provided.

The vehicle or receptacle used for carrying poultry must be thoroughly clean.

They may not be tied or bound by the neck, leg or wing; be lifted or carried by the head, neck, wing or tail or carried in a sack or bag and they must not be overcrowded.

The birds must be inspected at regular intervals and not be allowed to escape or fall out of the vehicle or a receptacle in which they are being carried.

A receptacle containing 50 birds or more must be labelled or marked showing its upright position and also a statement or symbol indicating that it is carrying poultry.

No substances of a solid, gaseous or liquid nature, goods, articles or equipment which could cause injury or suffering must be placed anywhere near poultry in a vehicle. Other creatures hostile to poultry may not travel with them and dead birds must not be loaded with live ones and any that die whilst in transit must be removed as soon as possible.

Drivers have to keep a record of movements in a format similar to that detailed in the regulations. The record must be kept in the vehicle and be made available for inspection by an authorised person (including a veterinary inspector) or a police constable, on demand.

A record is not required if the consignment being carried is of less than 50 birds.

An offence is committed if any of the requirements of the regulations are not complied with.

CARRIAGE OF RADIOACTIVE SUBSTANCES

Persons engaged in the handling and transporting of radioactive material must observe the following:

- The Radioactive Substances Act 1948
- Radioactive Substances (Carriage by Road) (Great Britain) Regulations 1974
- Ionising Radiations Regulations 1985.

Vehicles engaged in the carrying of this type of material must display the prescribed "Radioactive" notice at the front and rear and in addition a notice in the prescribed form must be posted in the cab of the vehicle visible to the driver.

CARRIAGE OF DANGEROUS SUBSTANCES IN ROAD TANKERS AND TANK CONTAINERS — WARNING PANELS

Road tankers and tank containers (containers with a capacity in excess of 3 cubic metres) carrying dangerous substances must display hazard warning panels and, where more than one type of dangerous substance is carried, compartment labels.

The requirements are contained in The Dangerous Substances (Conveyance by Road in Road Tankers and Tank Containers) Regulations 1981 (SI 1981 No. 1059).

Three panels have to be displayed on each tanker — one at the rear of the vehicle or tank and the others placed one on each side and as near to the front of the tank as possible. The lower edge of each panel must be at least 1m from the ground and the panel must be in an upright position. In addition where more than one type of substance is being transported compartment labels must be fixed one on each side and as near to the centre of each compartment as possible.

Warning panels (see pages 194 and 195) must show: the emergency action code for the particular substance) the substance identification number or, if more than one load is being carried, the word MULTI-LOAD; the appropriate hazard warning sign and the telephone number or other text indicating where specialist advice can be obtained. In addition the name or names of the substance and the name of the manufacturer or owner or his house symbol may also be shown.

Compartment labels must show the appropriate substance identification number and if possible the name of the substance and the appropriate hazard warning sign if different from the other hazard warning signs.

When delivery has been completed and the tank and/or compartments(s) have been emptied, cleaned or purged of the substance or vapour the warning panels and/or compartment labels should be removed or covered either completely or to the extent that only the telephone number, etc remains visible.

Responsibilities
It is the driver's responsibility to see that the warning panels and compartment labels, if applicable, are displayed correctly and that they are kept clean and free from obstruction. It is the employer's responsibility to see that the driver is made aware of the significance of the load and that the correct warning

panels are supplied, and he must provide full written information on the identity of the substance being carried and the
action to take in an emergency ("Tremcards" [Transport
Emergency Cards] are widely used). This information must be
kept in the driver's cab throughout the journey but once the
substance has been unloaded or discharged it should be
destroyed or removed from the vehicle or, alternatively,
placed in a securely closed container clearly marked to the
effect that the information is no longer applicable.

The employer must provide drivers with adequate instruction and training in the carrying of dangerous substances and
the action to take in emergencies and ensure that the driver is
fully conversant with the requirements and duties under these
regulations.

He must keep a record of the instruction and training given
and make a copy available to the driver if he requests it.

Fire extinguishers

All vehicles carrying dangerous substances must be equipped
with a suitable fire extinguisher capable of dealing, in the first
instance, with a fire in the engine.

An extinguisher able to deal with a fire in the load should
also be carried but expert advice on the type of extinguisher
required should first be obtained.

Fighting a fire in the load should not be attempted by anyone
unfamiliar in dealing with such situations. Call the emergency
services for assistance.

Parking

If the substance being carried displays the letter "E" in the
emergency action code or 1270 or 1268 as the substance identification number, the driver must ensure that when the vehicle
is parked it is in a safe place or is being supervised either by the
driver himself or some other competent person over the age of
18.

The Health and Safety Executive is responsible for enforc-
ing these regulations.

Rectangular Warning Panels

1. Type of panel required for **single loads**
   (all dimensions are given in millimetres).

2. Type of panel required for **multi-loads.**
   (See also *Compartment labels* below).

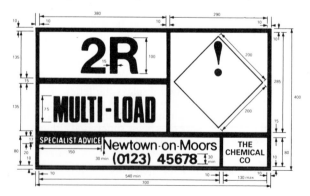

3. Compartment labels for **multi-loads.**

Colour of hazard warning panels and labels

Orange background (to BSS No. 381C (1980) No. 557 light orange) except the space for the hazard warning sign which must be *white*. Borders, internal dividing lines, letters and figures must be *black* but where in column three of the approved list a letter is shown as a white letter on a black background it shall be displayed as an *orange* letter on a black rectangle having a height and width of 10mm greater than the height and width of the letter respectively.

CARRIAGE OF DANGEROUS SUBSTANCES IN PACKAGES

In addition to the tanker regulations two other sets of regulations cover dangerous substances carried in **packaged** form and these are

- The Classification, Packaging and Labelling of Dangerous Substances Regulations 1984.
- The Road Traffic (Carriage of Dangerous Substances in Packages, etc) Regulations 1986.

The first set of regulations is concerned with the packaging and labelling of substances classified as dangerous and it is the duty of the supplier or consignor of such goods to ensure that they are correctly packed and labelled in accordance with the

Approved List ("Information Approved for the Classification, Packaging and Labelling of Dangerous Substances (2nd Edition))"

The second set of regulations cover

(a) any quantity of a dangerous substance in bulk;
(b) any quantity of any organic peroxide or any flammable solid (irrespective of its packing group if any) which is subject to the provisions of regulations 10(2) or 10(3) of these regulations;
(c) any organic peroxide (other than (b) above) or any flammable or toxic gas or any dangerous substance within packing group 1 of the "Approved List" (as mentioned above), or in Schedule 1 of these regulations, contained in a receptacle with a capacity of 5 litres or more;
(d) asbestos or asbestos waste which is a dangerous substance, in a receptacle with a capacity of 5 litres or more;
(e) hazardous waste designated as "special waste" by Regulation 2(1) of the Control of Pollution (Special Waste) Regulations 1980, in a receptacle with a capacity of 5 litres or more;
(f) any other dangerous substance in a receptacle with a capacity of 200 litres or more

and apply to any vehicle and any freight container used for the carriage of such substances from the commencement of loading to final unloading and if necessary until the vehicle or container has been cleaned so that no risk to health or safety remains.

Responsibilities

The operator must receive from the consignor or supplier full and accurate details of the type of substance to be carried, etc., and these must be passed on to the driver, in writing, together with information on any hazards which the substance may create and the action the driver must take in the event of an emergency. "Tremcards" (Transport Emergency Cards) are commonly used for this purpose but any form of written information is acceptable

It is the responsibility of the driver to keep this information in the vehicle in a safe but easily accessible place whilst the substance, or substances, are being carried and to make it available should any emergency arise.

When the substance(s) have been unloaded the driver should either destroy the information, remove it from the vehicle or place it in a securely closed container marked to the effect that it no longer applies.

When carrying organic peroxides or certain flammable solids special care must be taken to ensure that they do not overheat.

Driver training

It is a requirement of the law that drivers receive proper training in the handling of dangerous substances, etc, and fully understand the hazards that may arise. They must know what action to take in the event of an emergency.

The operator must keep records of training undertaken by drivers especially where the driver handles loads totalling 3 tonnes or more and for organic peroxides and self reactive flammable solids. A copy of the record of training must be made available to the driver.

Vehicle plates

Two rectangular reflectorised orange coloured plates (400mm long×300mm high) with a black border not more than 15mm wide, must be prominently displayed on the vehicle, one at the front and the other at the rear, when carrying a total quantity of 500 kilograms or more of one or more dangerous substances eg in receptacles of 5 litres capacity in Packing Group (PG)I, or receptacles of 200 litres capacity in PGII.

The plates must be kept clean and free from obstruction. They should be **removed** or **completely covered** when the vehicle ceases to carry a substance subject to the regulations in quantities below that mentioned above.

Parking and supervision

The driver is responsible for ensuring that a vehicle carrying dangerous goods when not being driven is parked in a safe place or it is being supervised at all times by him or some other competent person over the age of 18.

Fire extinguishers
A fire extinguisher capable, in the first instance, of dealing with an engine fire must be carried on the vehicle.

It is also advisable to carry an extinguisher able to fight a fire in the load but expert advice should be sought about the nature of the substance being carried and the type of extinguisher best able to deal with such an eventuality.

Preliminary fire fighting should only be carried out by drivers trained in the correct use of fire fighting equipment especially when this involves the load. Contact should be made to the emergency services as soon as possible as they will have the equipment and expertise necessary to deal with the incident.

Information to be made available
Information and any documents, etc., relating to the load being carried must be made available on request to a police officer or Department of Transport examiner.

"Approved Code of Practice"
An "Approved Code of Practice" is available covering the operational provisions of these regulations and gives practical guidance on the methods of compliance.

CARRIAGE OF SAND, BALLAST AND READY-MIXED CONCRETE

General
The carriage, handling and sale of these aggregates come under the Weights and Measures Act 1985, and the carriage by road is subject to certain requirements.

When ballast is carried in a road vehicle on a highway for delivery to a buyer and has been sold or will be sold by volume or by net weight, then the person in charge of the vehicle must be given a document signed by or on behalf of the seller, stating:

(a) the name and address of the seller

(b) the name and address of the buyer and the address to which the ballast is to be delivered

(c) the type of ballast

(d) the quantity of ballast, either by net weight or by volume

(e) sufficient particulars to identify the vehicle

(f) the place, date and time of the loading of the ballast in the vehicle.

Ballast may only be sold by volume in metric measurement.

Ballast is:

(a) sand, gravel, shingle, ashes and clinker of any decription

(b) broken slag, slate chippings and other stone chippings, granite chippings, etc (including such materials which have been coated with tar, bitumen or cement)

(c) any other material commonly used in the building and engineering industries as hard core or an aggregate.

No article may be used as a cubic measure of ballast other than a receptacle which conforms with the official requirements as to form, capacity, calibration, etc, but each receptacle may form part of a vehicle.

In measuring ballast against a calibration mark, all parts of the receptacle must be filled and the ballast levelled off against the calibration mark.

Safety precautions

Various types of vehicle bodies may be used for the transporting of sand and ballast but mainly the "tipper" type body is utilised.

Very seldom, if at all, are the loads covered, although the various granular materials carried are very much subject to movement in transit. Materials such as shingle and flint chippings become particularly hazardous in transit as they are constantly falling from the vehicle and can be a nuisance and danger to other road users. It is, of course, an offence to allow **any** load to endanger other road users and the law requires that sheeting or some other restraint be used to avoid this happening.

Vehicles employed in the carriage of sand, ballast and ready-mixed concrete, are, by the nature of their work, subject to

199

much greater stress and strain than other commercial vehicles. Except perhaps for ready-mixed concrete vehicles, all loading and unloading invariably takes place off the road where overwork and strain on steering, suspensions, clutch, engines and tyres are very much a common occurrence.

Loading and some discharging is usually carried out by mechanical means such as "shovels" and "grabbers", which play havoc with vehicle bodies and suspensions.

In the interest of courtesy and safety, particular attention should be paid to the following.

1. **Maintenance,** particularly "preventive" and "planned" maintenance must be conducted to a very high standard. Vehicle washing and cleaning facilities are essential if faults on chassis and components are to be easily detected.

2. **Vehicle bodies** should be well maintained to secure the loads and prevent material dripping on the roads, thus becoming a hazard to other road users.

3. **Drivers** should exercise caution when driving on the highway, around bends and on motorways at speed.

4. **Tyres** — particular attention should be paid to inspection and checking of tyres owing to the off the road conditions and the damage that can be caused by stones and flints, etc.

The vehicle operators in this industry are usually *owner-drivers* to whom the loss of a vehicle would mean total loss of income. Therefore, the aforementioned information should be of particular concern.

HEALTH AND SAFETY

First-Aid equipment

Drivers working with dangerous tools or equipment, travelling for long distances in remote areas, or those working alone in remote areas (eg some quarries, forestry or agricultural locations) where first-aid facilities are not readily available should carry a first-aid kit in the vehicle for use in emergencies.

The kit should comprise the following basic items —

adhesive dressings
triangular sterile bandage
6 safety pins
medium dressings

Kits should be checked periodically to ensure that the contents have not deteriorated. Items which have been used should be replaced as soon as possible.

Operating in dock areas

Drivers operating in dock areas especially those involving roll-on/roll-off ferries, straddle carriers, and other areas which may pose a hazard must wear high visibility clothing ie jacket, waistcoat, belt or sash, whenever they have to get out of their cab including when on the vehicle deck of a ferry. Protective head gear must also be worn if operations take them into areas where there is a risk of danger from above eg where loose cargos etc, are handled.

Drivers must not remain in the cab of their vehicle when parked on a straddle carrier grid and a container is being lifted on or off the vehicle.

ABANDONED MOTOR VEHICLES

It is an offence to abandon a motor vehicle, either on or off the highway. Fines can be imposed and in the case of a subsequent offence, the result can be either fines or a period of imprisonment.

Both the police and the local authorities are empowered to remove vehicles which are broken-down, causing an obstruction or appear to have been abandoned.

The regulations also include a scale of charges for the removal of a vehicle which has been illegally or obstructively parked. Currently these are:

For removal in London (other than motorways) £85
For removal elsewhere £85
For removal from a motorway £85
For removal from a loading area in London £85
For removal from a loading area elsewhere £85
Storge, each 24 hours or part thereof £12
Disposal £50

These charges have nothing to do with fixed penalty or excess charges, where appropriate, as these are a separate payment.

In areas where the use of wheel clamping is authorised a fee of £32 is charged for the release of a vehicle from a wheel clamp.

The police or local authority who have removed a vehicle illegally or obstructively parked etc, may retain custody of it until the charges have been paid.

AUTOMATIC LEVEL CROSSINGS

Additional safeguards have been introduced at automatic half-barrier level crossings and these are well covered by early warning road signs.

The action which should be taken is set out below:

1. At the crossing with automatic lifting barriers a vehicle **must not cross** the railway lines once the twin red warning lights have begun to flash.

2. Drivers should **never** zig-zag round the barriers when they are down.

3. When the barriers stay down and the red lights continue to flash after a train has gone, it means that another train is coming.

4. **Do not** enter the area marked on the road by yellow lines unless certain that there is enough clear road beyond the crossing for the vehicle and any overhanging load.

5. Always keep a reasonable distance from the vehicle in front.

6. If the vehicle stalls on the crossing the driver should get out together with any passengers and get clear of the crossing. He should **not waste time** and when clear should telephone the signalman immediately.

Special vehicles
If driving a vehicle which, with a trailer and its load, is more than 55 feet long, or more than 9 feet 6 inches wide, or more than 32 tonnes in weight or one that is unlikely to cross at more than 5 mph, the driver **must**:

(a) telephone the signalman and get permission to cross
(b) stop the vehicle at the "blue" traffic sign where a free telephone is installed.

After crossing the driver should stop at the telephone sign found usually 75 to 200 yards beyond the crossing and **inform the signalman that the crossing is clear.**

High and low vehicles
Where there are overhead cables a sign indicating this will be seen at early approach to the crossing. If the vehicle and its load is higher than 16 feet 6 inches (5.03m) no attempt should be made to cross.

Drivers of vehicles with low-load trailers should not cross an automatic half-barrier crossing until they have made absolutely sure that there is no risk of grounding. Where there is a danger of this a descriptive sign will be displayed at the approach to the crossing.

Remember that in the case of a special vehicle, permission must be obtained from the signalman to cross. Failure to do so can lead to a "totting-up" offence with endorsement and possible loss of licence.

HINTS AND TIPS

1. The qualities of a good driver are only demonstrated by remembering early teaching and continuing to apply the methods taught.

   Experience will come only through further driving and a determination to continue as started and not let any bad habits develop through slackness.

2. The successful driver, after passing the LGV driving test, must remember that he is joining the ranks of professionals who are skilled drivers and proud of their reputation. *One driver, indifferent to his obligations, can easily let the whole side down.*

3. Accident damage, coupled with vehicle loss of use can be expensive and harmful to the company's reputation. *Employers cannot afford to employ accident-prone drivers.*

4. It is essential that drivers show courtesy to other road users, customers and suppliers in the course of their duties. Any discourtesy on the part of the driver usually reflects on the employer.

5. Drivers should not "bunch" when driving on the highway, particularly on motorways, as the accident rate with this type of incident is very high.

   It is important to remember the braking and stopping distances and leave ample room between vehicles.

6. It is important to use the driving mirrors and ensure that they are always kept clean and are properly adjusted.

7. Yellow hatched boxes (BOX JUNCTIONS) are painted on the road at many congested road junctions. It is an offence to enter the "box" unless the exit is clear. A vehicle may halt in the box to make a right turn.

8. Drivers should know the one-way traffic sytems, particularly "in" and "out" of railway stations and goods yards as this will improve routeing and delivery times.

9. Drivers should always co-operate with the police, particularly in connection with town deliveries where "No Parking" prohibitions are concerned.

Contrary to the opinions of many drivers, much valuable assistance with delivery problems can be obtained in this way.

10. Pay particular attention to the securing of and the handling of vehicles with "high loads". Obtain from the employer the instruction sheet issued by user organisations. New bridges have a standard minimum height limit of 5.03m (16′ 6″) which means that a vehicle carrying a high load etc, must be below this limit to ensure safe passage. There are also many bridges having lower height limits and these are usually signed either at the approach to the bridge or on the bridge itself. A red triangular warning sign (enclosing figures) indicates maximum headroom available, a regulatory sign (red circle enclosing figures on a white ground) indicates that vehicles exceeding the height stated are prohibited.

Fines with possible licence endorsement and disqualification from driving faces the driver whose vehicle or load strikes a bridge.

11. Drivers found guilty of having unsafe loads can be fined up to £2000 and can also be charged with "careless driving". If the overall height of the vehicle and load exceed 3.66m a notice must be displayed in the cab showing the maximum overall height.

12. An offence is committed if the vehicle makes excessive noise. This applies to the load as well as the vehicle.

13. Drivers should check lights regularly. Spare bulbs should be carried for all the lamps on the vehicle. It is also a requirement of the law that all obligatory lamps (including reflectors) must be kept **clean** and in good working order. Likewise obligatory rear markings (where required) must be maintained in a **clean** and **efficient** condition.

14. Loading time **is not** driving time.

15. It is important to drive through the gears not on the brakes.

PART FOUR
INTERNATIONAL JOURNEYS

DRIVING ON THE CONTINENT

The procedure for driving on the Continent is much the same as for driving in the United Kingdom except that driving on the **right** of the road with right-hand steering calls for greater concentration and observation when overtaking.

A few rules of the road common to most continental countries must be observed. There are enforced priorities whereby drivers must give way to traffic approaching from the right and at roundabouts. The rules refer only to towns and suburban areas, and not to open roads or motorways (except at roundabouts). Most particularly, in respect of *white lines*, extreme care must be taken not to infringe any regulation as such misdemeanours can (and often do) result in the strictest of penalties being imposed.

Take suitable precautions when stopping

When driving on the right-hand side of the road, especially at night, caution should be exercised when making stops for refuelling and refreshment. Endeavour to select a site on the right-hand side of the road so that, when driving away, you automatically join the right-hand stream of traffic. If necessity dictates that a stop be made on the left-hand side of the road (normally, this is illegal) it is quite easy, by lapse of memory, to make the mistake of turning *left* against the oncoming traffic. This reference might appear to be frivolous but is included as a necessary caution against the many serious accidents which in the past *have* been caused in this manner.

Drivers must remember that a right-hand drive vehicle on the *right* of the road presents the same problem as does a left-hand drive vehicle being driven on the *left* in the United Kingdom. Caution therefore is all-important with especially careful use of the mirror when about to overtake or alter course. Direction indicators must be used — so make sure that

206

these (together with rear and stop lights) are in efficient working order.

When overtaking remember that, by the time the driver is in a position to observe oncoming traffic, the greater part of the vehicle will be exposed towards the crown of the road.

Spare light bulbs
Lights must be maintained in good working order at all times and in some countries defective lighting can incur heavy on-the-spot fines. A complete set of spare bulbs should therefore be carried on the vehicle.

Snow chains
Snow chains must be carried during winter months when travelling in Austria, Czechoslovakia, Finland, France (especially in the Vosges, Jura and Savior regions), Norway and Switzerland.

Fines
On-the-spot fines are usually imposed in most countries for incorrect documentation, drivers' hours offences, speeding and other traffic infringements.

Accident procedure
In the event of an accident drivers should be especially careful in exchanging particulars with third parties, particularly if their knowledge of the language is poor. The Michelin guide, or RAC and AA Continental Breakdown Services invariably have English-speaking staff who may be able to help. (It is quite possible that the breakdown services will be needed.) Drivers should carry a continental service kit, obtainable from vehicle manufacturers and agents.

In most countries in Europe a warning triangle must be carried for use in an emergency. The triangle must be placed in a prominent position some distance behind the vehicle or obstruction to warn approaching traffic. In Spain two warning triangles are required, one being placed 30m in front of the vehicle and the other 100m to the rear. Yugoslavia also requires two triangles when a vehicle is towing a trailer.

In addition to triangles vehicles exceeding 3.5t. total laden weight must carry wheel chocks (at least two) when travelling in Austria.

Hazard warning lights should also be used in emergencies.

It is also compulsory in most countries in Europe for vehicles to be equipped with a first-aid kit (Germany requires that a first-aid kit must include seamless disposable vinyl gloves which must be large size and interchangeable for either left or right handed users).

When travelling in Spain a "bail bond" should be obtained in case a driver is involved in an accident.

Accidents in Spain can have serious consequences and a driver, even though it may not be his fault, can be detained and his vehicle seized.

A "bail bond" is a written guarantee that a sum of money (usually up to £1,000) will be paid into a Spanish court as surety for bail.

This bond should be obtained when applying for the international certificate of insurance (Green Card) — see also page 209.

A vehicle nationality plate, ie "GB" plate must be displayed at the rear of the vehicle.

REGULATIONS AND PERMITS

Those intending to operate vehicles on continental services should have a full appreciation of the procedure so that delays, complications and unnecessary expenses do not arise.

The main requirements are: documentation; permits; knowledge of regulations and taxes; and it is considered most necessary that both fleet users and drivers are aware of their respective responsibilities.

Documents

Driving Licences: British driving licences or the new EC style unified driving licences are acknowledged in many, although not all, western European countries. An International

Driving Permit should therefore be obtained (either from the AA or RAC) unless it is certain that the British driving licence is valid.

Full Passports: These are essential in all countries.

Visas: These are not necessary for western Europe but are required for some east European and Middle Eastern countries. Application should be made to the respective embassies in this country.

Customs documentation
1. Vehicle:
     (a) Vehicle registration document (Form V5) — original, and
     (b) Carnet de Passage en Douane (if required — see page 210), is available from the motoring organisations.

2. Goods:
     (a) TIR Carnet (not EC Member States) or
     (b) ATA Carnet (see page 212)
     (c) Community transit document for EC countries.

Insurance
1. **Vehicle:** An international certificate of insurance (Green Card) should be obtained from operators' motor vehicle insurers.

2. **Driver:** A sickness policy to cover the driver whilst he is out of the country should also be considered. Leaflet SA28, available from the Department of Social Security, gives details of medical treatment available in EC countries. Form E111 must be carried to obtain treatment, etc whilst abroad.

3. **Bail Bond:** for journeys in Spain.

Permits
Permits for commercial vehicles are required in certain countries in Europe, namely, Austria*, Czechoslovakia, France*, Germany*, Hungary*, Italy*, Portugal*, Spain,

* hire and reward operations only.

Turkey, USSR and Yugoslavia and can be obtained from the International Road Freight Office (IRFO), Westgate House, Westgate Road, Newcastle-upon-Tyne NE1 1TW (Tel: 091 261 0031, Telex: 53351). Permits must be carried on the vehicle.

Applications should be made well in advance of the date of the intended journey and the fee for one journey permit (outward and return counts as one journey) is currently £2. Where permits allow more than one journey the cost is £1 per journey.

It is an offence for vehicles destined for France, Germany, Austria and/or Italy to leave the United Kingdom unless a valid permit has been issued authorising entry into these countries. The operator can be liable to a fine if he contravenes this regulation. Furthermore, the driver can be fined if he obstructs or refuses to comply with instructions given by a Department of Transport examiner. The examiner can prohibit the vehicle from leaving the United Kingdom if he considers the regulations are not being compiled with.

Carnet de Passage en Douane

This document covers the movement of vehicles and trailers and at present is required when entering the following countries — Iran, Iraq, Jordan, Kuwait, Lebanon, Saudi Arabia, Syria and Turkey. France requires them only for trailers/semi-trailers which have **not** been plated; Italy if vehicles are likely to remain for more than three months; Portugal for vehicles remaining in the country more than one month.

The Carnet is available from either the AA or the RAC.

TIR Carnet

Transports Internationale Routiers (TIR) have been assigned for the purpose of facilitating the speedy movement of goods by road transportation. The Carnets operate under international customs agreement for all countries who are signatories to the Geneva agreement. Therefore, possession of a TIR Carnet exempts a carrier from all normal examinations at frontiers throughout the journey, except for initial and final customs clearance inspections. The procedure also eliminates payment of deposits, duties and taxes and customs en route, except in certain cases.

TIR Carnets are obtained in this country through the Freight Transport Association and the Road Haulage Association.

There are, of course, specific requirements laid down for the holders of these Carnets regarding terms of operation, records, insurance and renewal.

Carnets are issued in booklet form, either of 14 or 20 volet and in these must be listed full particulars of the goods to be carried.

Full details of costs, etc are available from the associations.

The use of vehicles under TIR Carnet calls for certain requirements.

1. Construction of the body and fitting have to follow an international specification.

2. Before the vehicle can be used it must be inspected by a Department of Transport vehicle examiner and, if the vehicle complies with the regulations laid down, a certificate will be issued.

   Certain sectional photographs are also required and should always be carried with the certificate on the vehicle and made available for inspection by any customs officers.

3. TIR plates must be carried. These plates must also conform to regulations — they must measure 250mm x 400mm, have *white* letters "TIR" on a *blue* background and must be affixed to both front and rear of the vehicle.

   Plates are obtainable from the associations mentioned earlier in this chapter or from the vehicle builders.

4. In certain cases markings are required such as unladen and laden weights in kilograms as well as conventional references. These invariably are required with vehicles carrying bulk liquids.

TIR Carnets cannot be used for journeys to or within EC Member States.

Community Transit system
The European Community Transit System must be used for the movement of goods to and from Common Market coun-

tries and the Single Administrative Document (SAD) must accompany the goods to final destination.

Customs Notices Nos. 750, 750A and 751 explain the procedure to be adopted and can be obtained from Customs Offices.

ATA Carnet (Carnet de Passage en Douane pour l'Admission Temporaire)

The ATA Carnet is an International Customs Clearance Document allowing both personally accompanied and unaccompanied specified goods to be temporarily imported without payment of customs duty, or deposit, or bond. It is valid for 12 months.

This Carnet covers the temporary importation of (a) samples; (b) professional equipment; and (c) goods for exhibitions and fairs.

It is accepted in the following countries: Austria; Belgium; Bulgaria; Czechoslovakia; Denmark; Finland; France, Germany; Gibraltar; Greece; Hungary; Iran; the Irish Republic; Israel; Italy; Luxembourg; the Netherlands; Norway; Poland; Portugal; Rumania; Spain; Sweden; Switzerland; Turkey; the United Kingdom; Yugoslavia.

Applications for the Carnet should be made to the major Chambers of Commerce from whom full particulars are available.

Traffic regulations and taxes

The movement of commercial vehicles is prohibited or restricted in some Continental countries during weekends and public holidays, notably; Austria (also during any night); Czechoslovakia; France; Germany; Greece; Hungary; Italy; Spain; Sweden; (Rumania — May to September); Switzerland (also during any night) and Yugoslavia.

In accordance with United Kingdom adherence to the relevant International Taxation Convention and agreements with certain countries, goods vehicles registered in the United Kingdom are not subject to vehicle tax whilst travelling in: Austria; Belgium; Bulgaria; Czechoslovakia; Denmark; Fin-

Model

RNA
5 - 1992

the figures denote month and year of expiry.

Colours: capital Latin letters, at least 100mm high, in dark blue on a white ground.

Note: the mark (***) must be affixed to "thin side walls" equipment which has been satisfactorily tested, below the designated mark.

Vehicles with thin side walls used for carrying frozen and deep frozen foodstuffs to and from Italy have to be specially tested and certificated to ensure that they comply with Articles 2 and 4 of the Agreement made in Paris on 24.6.86.

The certificate should be carried by the driver when the foodstuffs are transported throughout their journey by road and no trans-loading takes place. If other forms of transport are used the certificate should be held by the operator.

The following countries have acceded to this agreement:

Austria, Belgium, Bulgaria, Denmark, Finland, France, Germany, Italy, Luxembourg, Morocco, the Netherlands, Norway, Portugal, Spain, Sweden, Switzerland, the United Kingdom, the USSR and Yugoslavia.

DANGEROUS GOODS

The transporting of dangerous goods to and from the Continent of Europe is covered by the European Agreement for the International Carriage of Dangerous Goods by Road (short title — ADR).

This Agreement is backed by a number of European countries (parties to the Agreement) who undertake to permit the transport of dangerous goods by road through their territories. The contracting parties are: Austria, Belgium, Denmark, Finland, France, Germany, Hungary, Italy, Luxembourg, the Netherlands, Norway, Poland, Portugal, Spain, Sweden, Switzerland, the United Kingdom and Yugoslavia.

Examination (in the United Kingdom) of the vehicle and of the tank, if fitted to it, is carried out by separate authorities. Examination of the vehicle itself is carried out by DTp examiners at large goods vehicle testing stations.

Appointments for vehicle examinations follow a similar procedure as for testing, but the test is in addition to the normal testing examination.

The fee for an ADR examination is extra to the testing fee.

Requirements

Inspection of tanks takes into account the peculiar commodities likely to be carried and they are tested for corrosion, cracking at attachment points, seams and valve connections.

Safety precautions must be taken regarding construction and fittings such as:

(a) wiring circuits and electrical equipment to be protected from overloading

(b) positioning of the exhaust and fuel tank

(c) two fire extinguishers (although this is a domestic requirement it is advisable to carry fire extinguishers in Germany having at least 10kg capacity) must be carried, one suitable for dealing with engine fires and the other for fires in the load. A third extinguisher may also be carried on articulated vehicles, or those drawing trailers, so that an extinguisher is readily available to deal with a fire in the load on the trailer

(d) ADR vehicles must carry a tool-kit for emergency repairs, which must include a suitable chock (Germany requires at least two) for scotching the wheels

(e) on the Continent only, **two amber lights** of the continuous flashing type must be carried and these must operate independently of the vehicle's electrical system. These additional lights are for emergency purposes and should be placed on the road 10m in front and to the rear of the vehicle. (Lamps must be in good working order at all times.)

land; France; Germany; Hungary; the Irish Republic; Luxembourg; the Netherlands; Norway; Poland; Rumania; Sweden; Switzerland; USSR and Yugoslavia.

Austria, Norway, Rumania (if the vehicle exceeds a certain weight), Switzerland, Sweden and Turkey levy **road transport** taxes which are payable at the border.

Driver's hours and record keeping: see pages 37–38 and 53.

Duty-free fuel
Vehicles crossing between Member States of the EC are allowed at least 200 litres of fuel in their tanks duty-free. Vehicles entering Austria (not an EC member) are also allowed 200 litres of fuel duty-free.

CMR (Convention Merchandises Routiers)
This convention applies to contracts for the carriage of goods by road for reward when the place of taking over the goods and the place designated for delivery are situated in two different countries of which at least one is a contracting country.

The convention was given the force of law in the United Kingdom by the Carriage of Goods by Road Act 1965.

With the exception of Turkey and the USSR all countries in Europe are parties to the convention and when a carrier transports goods for reward a CMR consignment note should be completed and accompany the goods throughout the journey, irrespective of whether they are transported by one carrier or by a number of carriers.

PERISHABLE FOODSTUFFS (ATP)

The Agreement on the International Carriage of Perishable Foodstuffs and on the Special Equipment to be used for such Carriage (ATP — Accord Transports Perissables) applies to certain prescribed frozen foodstuffs, temperature conditions and standards of thermal efficiency required of equipment used for carrying such foodstuffs. It covers journeys made by road and rail and sea crossings of less than **150km** or by any combination thereof. It does not apply to domestic transport and air transport.

213

The prescribed foodstuffs and the temperatures at which they must be maintained during transportation are as follows.

Quick (deep)-frozen and frozen (Annex 2 of ATP):

Ice cream and concentrated fruit juices .... −20°C
Frozen or quick (deep)-frozen fish .... −18°C
All other quick (deep)-frozen foodstuffs .... −18°C
Butter and other frozen fats.................... −14°C
Frozen red offal, egg yolks, poultry and game ... −12°C
Frozen meat, all other frozen foodstuffs .... −10°C

A brief rise in temperature of 3°C maximum is allowed if caused by certain technical operations, eg defrosting of the mechanical refrigerated equipment.

Foodstuffs which are neither quick (deep)-frozen nor frozen (Annex 3 of ATP):

Red offal .... +3°C
Milk (raw or pasteurised) in tanks, for immediate
consumption .... +4°C
Industrial milk .... +6°C
Yoghurt, kefir, cream and fresh cheese .... +4°C

Maximum transit time should not exceed 48 hours' duration for the above items.

Meat products (except those stabilised by salting,
smoking, drying or sterilisation) .... +6°C
Butter.. +6°C
Game, poultry and rabbits .... +4°C
Meat, other than red offal .... +7°C
Fish, molluscs and crustaceans (other than smoked,
salted, dried or live fish, live molluscs and live
crustaceans) must always be carried in melting ice.

A certificate of conformity must be in force for equipment used for such operations and a designated mark fixed to the equipment during the validity of the certificate.

The designated mark (as prescribed in Annex 1, Appendix 4 to the Agreement) must be in the following form:

The prescribed foodstuffs and the temperatures at which they must be maintained during transportation are as follows.

Quick (deep)-frozen and frozen (Annex 2 of ATP):

Ice cream and concentrated fruit juices . . . . −20°C
Frozen or quick (deep)-frozen fish . . . . −18°C
All other quick (deep)-frozen foodstuffs . . . . −18°C
Butter and other frozen fats . . . . −14°C
Frozen red offal, egg yolks, poultry and game . . . . −12°C
Frozen meat, all other frozen foodstuffs . . . . −10°C

A brief rise in temperature of 3°C maximum is allowed if caused by certain technical operations, eg defrosting of the mechanical refrigerated equipment.

Foodstuffs which are neither quick (deep)-frozen nor frozen (Annex 3 of ATP):

Red offal . . . . +3°C
Milk (raw or pasteurised) in tanks, for immediate consumption . . . . +4°C
Industrial milk . . . . +6°C
Yoghurt, kefir, cream and fresh cheese . . . . +4°C

Maximum transit time should not exceed 48 hours' duration for the above items.

Meat products (except those stabilised by salting, smoking, drying or sterilisation) . . . . +6°C
Butter . . . . +6°C
Game, poultry and rabbits . . . . +4°C
Meat, other than red offal . . . . +7°C
Fish, molluscs and crustaceans (other than smoked, salted, dried or live fish, live molluscs and live crustaceans) must always be carried in melting ice.

A certificate of conformity must be in force for equipment used for such operations and a designated mark fixed to the equipment during the validity of the certificate.

The designated mark (as prescribed in Annex 1, Appendix 4 to the Agreement) must be in the following form:

Model

```
┌─────────┐
│   RNA   │      the figures denote month and year of
│         │      expiry.
│ 5 - 1992│
└─────────┘
```

Colours: capital Latin letters, at least 100mm high, in dark
blue on a white ground.

Note: the mark (***) must be affixed to "thin side walls"
equipment which has been satisfactorily tested, below
the designated mark.

Vehicles with thin side walls used for carrying frozen and
deep frozen foodstuffs to and from Italy have to be specially
tested and certificated to ensure that they comply with Articles
2 and 4 of the Agreement made in Paris on 24.6.86.

The certificate should be carried by the driver when the
foodstuffs are transported throughout their journey by road
and no trans-loading takes place. If other forms of transport
are used the certificate should be held by the operator.

The following countries have acceded to this agreement:

Austria, Belgium, Bulgaria, Denmark, Finland, France,
Germany, Italy, Luxembourg, Morocco, the Netherlands,
Norway, Portugal, Spain, Sweden, Switzerland, the United
Kingdom, the USSR and Yugoslavia.

DANGEROUS GOODS

The transporting of dangerous goods to and from the Continent of Europe is covered by the European Agreement for
the International Carriage of Dangerous Goods by Road
(short title — ADR).

This Agreement is backed by a number of European
countries (parties to the Agreement) who undertake to
permit the transport of dangerous goods by road through
their territories. The contracting parties are: Austria, Belgium, Denmark, Finland, France, Germany, Hungary, Italy,
Luxembourg, the Netherlands, Norway, Poland, Portugal,
Spain, Sweden, Switzerland, the United Kingdom and
Yugoslavia.

Examination (in the United Kingdom) of the vehicle and of the tank, if fitted to it, is carried out by separate authorities. Examination of the vehicle itself is carried out by DTp examiners at large goods vehicle testing stations.

Appointments for vehicle examinations follow a similar procedure as for testing, but the test is in addition to the normal testing examination.

The fee for an ADR examination is extra to the testing fee.

Requirements

Inspection of tanks takes into account the peculiar commodities likely to be carried and they are tested for corrosion, cracking at attachment points, seams and valve connections.

Safety precautions must be taken regarding construction and fittings such as:

(a) wiring circuits and electrical equipment to be protected from overloading

(b) positioning of the exhaust and fuel tank

(c) two fire extinguishers (although this is a domestic requirement it is advisable to carry fire extinguishers in Germany having at least 10kg capacity) must be carried, one suitable for dealing with engine fires and the other for fires in the load. A third extinguisher may also be carried on articulated vehicles, or those drawing trailers, so that an extinguisher is readily available to deal with a fire in the load on the trailer

(d) ADR vehicles must carry a tool-kit for emergency repairs, which must include a suitable chock (Germany requires at least two) for scotching the wheels

(e) on the Continent only, **two amber lights** of the continuous flashing type must be carried and these must operate independently of the vehicle's electrical system. These additional lights are for emergency purposes and should be placed on the road 10m in front and to the rear of the vehicle. (Lamps must be in good working order at all times.)

Handling and storage

Of the many provisions in the agreement, only a few of the essentials are listed.

1. The engine must be switched off during loading and unloading, *except* when used for pumping appliances with loading and discharging.
2. The mixing of certain loads in one transport unit or container is prohibited and there are no special provisions for cleaning before and after unloading.
3. Loads must be stowed and secured to prevent shifting or coming into contact with other parts of the load or sides of the vehicle.
4. With the carrying of mixed loads, dangerous substances must be separated from other packages.
5. Nothing may be loaded on top of a fragile package and the driver and his mate are prohibited from opening packages containing dangerous substances.

Markings

On the Continent vehicles carrying dangerous substances are required to display two rectangular orange coloured plates in reflex reflective material. These should be 40cm (16 inches) square, one fitted to the front and one to the rear of the vehicle. Vehicles engaged on international journeys travelling through the United Kingdom may display such a plate at the rear of the vehicle only.

Packaging and labelling

The labelling of different classes of substances is as listed in ADR regulations and dangerous goods accepted for international carriage must be labelled in accordance with these requirements.

Driver instruction

The employer is responsible for ensuring that drivers (and mates) receive thorough instruction relating to the requirements on the carriage of dangerous goods. For the benefit of drivers and particularly owner-drivers, a few of the essential instructions are listed.

1. A mate is obligatory when carrying Class 1 substances.

2. Crews must be instructed on the safety aspects of ADR vehicle movements which include:

   (a) a vehicle must not be parked in a built-up area

   (b) a vehicle must not be left without being under the supervision of the driver, his mate or some other fully trained person.

3. Crews must receive training in the action to be taken and treatment to be given:

   (a) in the event of persons coming into contact with the substance being carried

   (b) in the case of fire and, in particular, the type of extinguisher and contents to be used

   (c) in the case of breakage or deterioration of the packages or substances being carried, particularly when they have been spilled on the road.

4. In the event of a vehicle which is carrying a dangerous substance being halted on the road for some reason which the crew is unable to deal with quickly, they should notify the nearest competent authority. The driver must be issued with and carry at all times a list of the appropriate authorities.

   The carrying of passengers is forbidden.

A driver of a tank vehicle or transport unit carrying tanks or tank containers exceeding 3000 litres capacity must hold a certificate as proof that he has completed a course of training in the carrying of dangerous goods.

Note: as some European countries are insisting that drivers of any vehicle carrying dangerous substances show proof of training it is advisable to carry details of any training received.

Copies of the European Agreement concerning the international carriage of dangerous goods by road (ADR) may be purchased from HM Stationery Office.

INTERNATIONAL SERVICES

Tyre maintenance

Detailed requirements for the maintenance of tyres are covered under the appropriate heading on page 102, but there is some additional information relevant to continental operation, which may prove useful to those driving on the Continent.

When proceeding on continental journeys it is recommended that the following items be included in a vehicle service kit:

1. Tyre pressure gauge.
2. Box of Schrader valve cores.
3. Valve core key.

At the commencement of all continental journeys it is necessary to check and ensure that sound tyres with good treads (including a spare) are installed, as the servicing points on the Continent are less frequent than those in the United Kingdom. The cost in service, plus delay, can therefore be very high.

Service and supply

A "tyre breakdown service" is available in some European and Scandinavian countries — Belgium, Germany, Holland, Denmark, Finland, Norway and Sweden — for customers of members of the National Tyre Distributors Association (NTDA) in the United Kingdom.

In the event of a tyre failure the driver should contact his own company giving the following details:

(a) his location

(b) telephone number at which he can be contacted

(c) the tyre problem

(d) size, type and make of tyre

(e) make, colour, registration number of vehicle or trailer, etc.

The company should then contact NTDA at Broadway House, London SW19, (Tel: 081-540 3859) with the details so that action can be taken to call out a tyre specialist in the locality to effect the necessary repairs.

The cost of replacement tyres and any other work carried out will be invoiced through NTDA to the customer of the member.

Credit facilities for fuel supplies
Credit facilities for fuel supplies on the Continent of Europe are available through Shell UK Oil, in collaboration with Shell in Europe.

"Euro-Shell" is a scheme which provides a refuelling and lubrication service in Western Europe for haulage operators. Approved credit customers are issued with "Euro-Shell" service cards which enable their drivers to obtain fuel supplies, etc in Austria, Belgium, Denmark, Finland, France, Germany, Greece, Italy, Luxembourg, the Netherlands, Norway, Portugal, Sweden, Switzerland and Turkey without having to pay in local currencies.

Booklets listing international haulage service stations and maps showing their locations are issued with this service.

For details of the facilities offered contact should be made to the nearest Shell UK Oil Industrial Sales Regional Office.

Fuel injection service
If a vehicle breaks down with engine trouble it is possible that the fault would be somewhere in the fuel system. The failure might be in the fuel system of an auxiliary diesel engine driving a refrigeration unit, etc.

To assist operators of both goods and passenger vehicles fitted with Lucas equipment, the Lucas Group have published a booklet entitled *Lucas Service Products Support*. This lists servicing and parts supply agents throughout Europe for Lucas accessories and is available from CAV Ltd, Service Publications Dept, PO Box 36, Worple Way, Acton, London W3 7SS.

Rubery Owen-Rockwell running gears
Rubery Owen-Rockwell publish a service directory listing service points in Austria, Belgium, France, Italy, Luxembourg, the Netherlands and West Germany and all Scandinavian countries, for drivers of articulated vehicles, where services and parts can be obtained. The Directory is available from Rubery Owen-Rockwell Ltd, 1/3 Cranford Court, Hardwick Grange, Woolston, Warrington, Cheshire, (Tel: 0925 823023, Telex: 628056).

METRIC CONVERSION TABLES

Weight

(1 Imperial ton = 2,240 lb = 1,016 kg)
(1 Tonne   = 2,205 lb = 1,000 kg)
(1 Short ton   = 2,000 lb =   907 kg)

lb		kg
2.205	1	0.454
4.409	2	0.907
6.614	3	1.361
8.818	4	1.814
11.103	5	2.268
13.228	6	2.722
15.432	7	3.175
17.637	8	3.629
19.842	9	4.082
22.046	10	4.536
220.460	100	45.359
2204.600	1000	453.591

Length

(1000 mm = 39.275 in. = 3.28 ft)

in		m
9.843	¼	0.006
19.685	½	0.013
29.528	¾	0.019
39.370	1	0.025
78.740	2	0.051
118.110	3	0.076
157.480	4	0.102
196.850	5	0.127
236.220	6	0.152
275.691	7	0.178
314.961	8	0.203
354.331	9	0.229
393.701	10	0.254
433.071	11	0.279

Velocity

Expressed in Units per Hour
(1000 m = 1 km = 1,094 yds = 0.62 miles)

Miles		km
1	=	1.609
5	=	8.047
10	=	16.093
15	=	24.140
30	=	48.280
40	=	64.374
50	=	80.467
70	=	112.654

Area and Volume

(100 sq cm = 1 sq dcm   100 sq dcm = 1 sq m)
(100 cc.   = 1 cu dcm   100 cu dcm = 1 cu m)

1 sq in	=	6.45 sq cm
1 sq ft	=	9.3 sq dcm
1 sq yd	=	83.6 sq dcm
1 cu in	=	16.38 cc
1 cu ft	=	28.3 cu dcm
1 cu yd	=	765 cu dcm

PART FIVE

WEIGHBRIDGE SITES IN GB

The following is a list of Department of Transport dynamic axle weighbridges situated at various locations in Great Britain. Those that have a self-weigh facility in place or being installed are marked with an asterisk.

WEIGHBRIDGE SITES

North Eastern Traffic Area

A1 SCOTCH CORNER
Middleton Tyas
North Yorkshire

A19 WELLFIELD
Co. Durham

A1/A659 BOSTON SPA
Wetherby
West Yorks.

A63 SOUTH CAVE
North Humberside

Nepshaw Lane*
GILDERSOME
Morley

A1-Robin Hoods Well
SKELLOW
Doncaster

Blackley New Road
AINLEY TOP
Huddersfield

A61-Barnsley Road
TANKERSLEY
Barnsley

KING GEORGE V
DOCKS*
Kingston upon Hull
Humberside

Approach Road A15*
HUMBER BRIDGE
Hessle

North Western Traffic Area

A5 HOLYHEAD
Anglesey
North Wales

WALLASEY TUNNEL
(EAST)
Liverpool

WALLASEY TUNNEL
(WEST)
Liverpool

M62 MOTORWAY
(JCT 20)
THORNHAM

A59 SAMLESBURY
Nr Preston
Lancs.

A556 ROSTHERNE
Cheshire

A5117 XM56
DUNKIRK
Cheshire

A74 HARKER
CARLISLE
Cumbria

A494-EWLOE
Clwyd
North Wales

West Midlands
Traffic Area
A449 Link Road
WARNDON

A5-WALL ISLAND
Lichfield, Staffs

M6 MOTORWAY —
DOXEY
Nr Stafford

A45/M45 THURLESTON
ISLAND
(DUNCHURCH)
Rugby

M5-MOTORWAY (JCT 3)
QUINTON

A40*
Three Crosses
ROSS-ON-WYE

Eastern Traffic Area
(Nottingham)
A43 TOWCESTER
Northants

A17/A15 HOLDINGHAM
Sleaford
Lincs

A428/M1 (JCT 18) CRICK
Northants

A46/52 SAXONDALE
The Old Nottingham Road
BINGHAM, NOTTS

Eastern Traffic Area
(Cambridge)
Stone Grove Road*
The Dock
FELIXSTOWE
IP11 8SU

Old A45 Road
RISBY
Suffolk

A1 Southbound
Connington Fen
SAWTRY
Cambridgeshire

A1 Northbound
Lower Caldecote
SANDY
Bedfordshire

South Wales Traffic Area
A40 PENBLEWIN
Narberth
Dyfed

M4-MOTORWAY
   (COLDRA)
Newport, Gwent

Western Traffic Area
MILLBAY DOCKS*
Plymouth
Devon PL1 3EF

A303 WYLYE
WILTS

Off A361
SAMPFORD PEVERELL
Tiverton, Devon

Continental Freight*
Ferry Terminal
New Harbour Road
POOLE, Dorset
BH15 1BW

A38 Anchor Inn Lay-by
KENNFORD, Devon

A35 Lay-by
PUDDLETOWN
Dorchester, Dorset

A46 TORMARTON
Avon

Metropolitan Traffic Area
A30 STAINES BY-PASS

A414/M11 (JCT7) HARLOW
Essex

M25 MOTORWAY (JCT9)
   LEATHERHEAD
   INTERCHANGE
Surrey

A13 BARKING

A3 BURPHAM
Nr Guildford, Surrey

A1 HOLLOWAY ROAD

South Eastern Traffic Area
DOVER (EAST) DOCK*
Dover, Kent

A23 HANDCROSS*
West Sussex

Stockers Hill
BOUGHTON
Kent

A27 BEDDINGHAM
East Sussex

A26/A22 Junction
Millpond
Maresfield, East Sussex

A34/415 Junction
Marsham Road
ABINGDON
Oxon

A27 WITHY PATCH*
Lancing
West Sussex

DOVER (WEST) DOCK*
Kent

SHEERNESS DOCKS
Sheerness, Kent

PORSTMOUTH DOCKS*
Portsmouth, Hants

M1 MOTORWAY (JCT14)
NEWPORT PAGNELL
Bucks

Southlands Road
DENHAM

Scottish Traffic Area
A75 CASTLE KENNEDY

A90 CRAMOND*

A92 FINDON*
Nr Aberdeen

A74 BEATTOCK SUMMIT

M9 CRAIGFORTH
Stirling

Tayside Truckstop*
Smeaton Road
Dundee